AUTHENTIC
POWER

AUTHENTIC POWER

GIVE YOURSELF PERMISSION TO FEEL

ASHLEY BERNARDI

FOREWORD BY

EMMA SEPPÄLÄ, Ph.D.

THE
collective
BOOK STUDIO

Library of Congress Cataloging-in-Publication Data available.
ISBN: 978-1-951412-32-6
Ebook ISBN: 978-1-951412-74-6
LCCN: 2021902338

Manufactured in China.
Design by Andrea Kelly.

10 9 8 7 6 5 4 3 2 1

The Collective Book Studio
Oakland, California

FOR

Mike, Alyssa, Kate & Scarlet

CONTENTS

FOREWORD

I've spent years researching the science and psychology of how people can thrive and find happiness in meaning in the face of challenging emotional situations. Through several decades of research on human emotions, trauma, and well-being, I've seen firsthand that we can build emotional health. Post-traumatic growth is real.

No one goes through life without experiencing some form of emotional trauma—or multiple traumas. It can be a car accident, a sudden death in the family, loss of a job, social or peer rejection, a separation or divorce, balancing kids and work, or like a hurricane, flood, or pandemic. Emotional trauma is caused by an event that feels life-altering in some way. It's any experience that overwhelms your thoughts, emotions, or body, making you fear for your life or the life of another. Your fight-or-flight system (the sympathetic nervous system) is activated. And once you live with post-traumatic stress, you have a hard time turning it off: sleep challenges, recurring memories of the trauma, anxiety, depression, and irritability all make for an unhealthy and debilitating existence.

I can think of no better person than Ashley to communicate the tools to work through emotional pain and grief. She and I met years ago when I was launching my book. I was drawn to her seemingly boundless positive energy. We bonded over open discussions on emotional traumas. For Ashley, it was her father dying from a heart attack right in front of her at the tender age of eleven. The grief and guilt she carried for years created incredible emotional pain inside of her, which she avoided by overworking and overdrinking. The stress and anxiety that built up inside of Ashley by avoiding her feelings, coupled with her debilitating diagnosis of Lyme disease and postpartum depression, literally brought her to her knees.

I have seen firsthand how Ashley's commitment to a path of true healing through facing the mess inside has made her wiser, stronger, happier, and healthier. Her story will inspire you, and the expert advice she has gathered will give you techniques to find your own ability to heal from adversity.

Ashley's superpower is connection. She is a connector of people and ideas, and this book is the ultimate result of that. She's assembled wisdom and science on finding hope and healing from more than twenty experts in health, wellness, and nutrition—from an impressive list of people.

Ashley's ability to curate the best techniques comes from her skills honed as a renowned publicist and former journalist. She possesses a journalist's dedication to facts, a psychologist's belief in the power of emotional healing, and a compassionate heart for others.

The practices you'll find inside this book have been proven to help people survive, thrive, and grow in challenging emotional situations— practices such as showing compassion for yourself and others, spending time in nature, community service, and many others.

Life has a way of throwing things at us that turn our world upside down and our emotions into a messy state. Ashley gives you permission to authentically feel and heal, and her hand-selected tribe of experts will show you paths to renewed healing and hope.

—Emma Seppälä, Ph.D.

Lecturer at the Yale School of Management, Faculty Director of the Yale School of Management's Women's Leadership Program, Science Director of Stanford University's Center for Compassion and Altruism Research and Education, and author of *The Happiness Track*.

INTRODUCTION

I see you, friend. I know those feelings when something isn't going right, or maybe even terribly wrong.

Yet everyone expects you to be strong, not to crack, not to miss a beat. You hold it together on the outside, but inside you are hurting, feeling helpless, and losing hope you'll ever feel better again.

Everyone is going to grapple in their life with some form of emotional messiness based on a traumatic event, whether it's the painful death of a parent or loved one, the devastating end of a marriage, a debilitating health diagnosis, the loss of a job, or closure of a business. It's just part of being a human being on this planet.

Collectively, we have recently experienced a global trauma in the form of a pandemic. Witnessing millions of deaths, experiencing a huge economic jolt, and living with severe curbs on social interaction has had a marked effect on people's mental health. Numerous studies have shown up to 40 percent of people have suffered from anxiety and depression at various times due to the pandemic.

No matter how strong you think you are, life is just going to hand us things that make us feel anxious, sad, fearful, angry, or hopeless.

Your first reaction to these feelings may be like mine was—to try and push these messy critters back down inside to hold it together at work and at home. What I've learned over the years is that if I push these uncomfortable feelings and emotions back down inside me and ignore them, instead of truly feeling them and processing them, it will be at the cost of my health, livelihood, and well-being. I want you to know that it is okay not to have to buck up and try to be the strong one all the time. That it is okay to put your self-care first. These are the first steps to healing and owning your authentic power.

It may be hard to see at first, but having these confusing, dark, and even ugly emotions presents an extraordinary opportunity to search within, and to find the light and hope no matter how terrible, sad, and alone we may be feeling. I now see Lyme disease and postpartum depression as my greatest life lesson that jump-started the necessary work I needed to do to heal not just from this disease, but from the trauma that haunted my soul as a child.

As a publicist, I am fortunate and grateful to have access to many of the world's leading and up and coming experts in mind, body, and spiritual health. They have been my clients, and have become my friends. I've learned so much from each of them over the years, and I wanted to share their gifts with you in this book. I find myself turning often to the tried-and-true coping mechanisms that you'll find within these pages.

These incredible healers can help you, too, find the healing for your heart and reignite hope in your life. Of course, I understand that overcoming a serious trauma or debilitating emotions can also require the help of medical and psychological professionals, of which I am not. But I do know that the wisdom of the health and wellness experts found in these pages can help you lean into the power of hope, and discover the deepest and best parts of yourself, otherwise known as your authentic power.

I'd like you to consider a more conscious and mindful way to think about difficult experiences (which I often like to call "my mess"), and therefore, perhaps a greater capacity to process them and, in turn, anticipate and know that better things are to come. Getting to a place of hope requires deliberate actions, especially if you've experienced traumatic events and emotions.

My hope for you is that this book will inspire your journey to a healthier mind, body, and spirit, and to face the future with new hope and resilience.

THE EMOTIONAL TSUNAMI

"EMBRACE THE GLORIOUS MESS THAT YOU ARE."

-ELIZABETH GILBERT,
AUTHOR OF *EAT, PRAY, LOVE*

CHAPTER 1

YOU DON'T HAVE TO BE STRONG

How many times in your life have you been told that you are "so strong"?

You lose your job during a pandemic and cobble together freelance work to make ends meet. You are so strong.

You lose a loved one to an illness and plan the funeral. You are so strong.

You're a busy working mom of three kids juggling work and life with little time to care for yourself. You are so strong.

You're battling cancer, going through chemo, spending your days vomiting, losing your hair, and losing the ability to recognize yourself in the mirror.

And yet. And yet, you are "so strong."

My entire life, I've been told I am so strong.

I was so strong when I tried to save my dad's life when I was eleven, as he was suffering from a heart attack that left blood to his heart 90 percent blocked.

I was so strong when I was diagnosed with postpartum depression after my third child and put in a part-time mental health facility.

I was so strong when I suffered from a debilitating mystery illness that left me unable to care for my family.

But let's be honest. Did you feel strong despite people telling you how strong you were?

I didn't. Yet I thought I needed to wear my "strong" cape because since I was eleven, I was told I needed to be strong.

For years, I put on the facade that I thought people wanted to see of me: one of strength, an army colonel's daughter who attempted to save his life; and nearly twenty years later, a mother trying to do it all only to suffer from a mystery illness that nearly killed me. And to be perfectly honest, the mask of strength was what almost caused my demise, not the illness.

In my professional career of media relations and training, I often teach that "your mess is your masterpiece." But why don't we show it? Why don't we own our mess? Why do we put on the mask of strength despite feeling the exact opposite?

A messy brew of anxiety, fear, and even depression has stuck with me since the traumatic event of my father's death in childhood, as it has for my friend Lorilee Binstock. A survivor of childhood sexual abuse, Lorilee experienced multiple suicide attempts, and later, spent months in a treatment center away from her children and husband diving into holistic healing techniques to address her childhood trauma. She came out on the other side renewed, inspired, and healed. Now she hosts the wildly popular *A Trauma Survivor Thriver's Podcast* and has launched a magazine titled *Authentic Insider*.

Lorilee introduced me to Dr. Dale DeNunzio, a therapist who specializes in techniques to heal trauma. He explains that events that become "too much" for us—too intense or too unmanageable—create feelings that overwhelm our nervous system, which makes it difficult to process them. "It is important to remember that having trauma does not mean that someone is unfixable, broken, or wrong. They are wounded. Trauma actually comes from the Greek word for wound. We all have been wounded in our lives."

I lost my father to a sudden-death heart attack when I was eleven years old. My mother, my nine-year-old sister, Alexandra, and I were all home when it happened, and he died right before our eyes. It was a Sunday evening, and we had just finished watching a family movie, *Jaws*. My dad was especially tired that evening and went up to bed. I put my pajamas on and went to give him a kiss goodnight. "I love you, daddy," I said as I kissed him on the cheek. "I love you, too, honey," he replied. Those were the last words we ever spoke to each other.

Moments later, as my mom was tucking me into bed, we heard moaning coming from my parents' room. My mom rushed to his side and started screaming, "Jimmy! Jimmy!" He was unresponsive. The moaning continued. For some reason, I had the sense to run down to my dad's office where we kept the house phone, and dialed 911. My fingers fumbled over the numbers, and the first time I tried, I didn't get through. I tried again. I continued to hear frantic screaming coming from my parents' room, and, at that point, my sister, who was just nine years old, rushed to my mom's side to help. I didn't know it at the time, but my sister started administering CPR on my dad while my mom stood by her side in shock. My dad and sister had just happened to take a CPR class together a week prior at the insistence of my mother. I was trying to get help. I reached the 911 operator and tried to explain that my dad was in distress, and that he needed help. I gave them our address and they said they were on the way. I'm not sure if the operator suggested what to do next or if it was my own idea, but I ran out the door in my pajamas to get help. We lived in a four-house pipestem, so I immediately turned to my neighbors on the right and banged on their door. They answered (thankfully) moments later, and rushed to be with my mom and sister.

After that, it was a blur. An ambulance came. The paramedics pulled my sister off of my dad to take over CPR, and she ran and hid in a closet with our dog and cried. I was shuttled to another neighbor's house with kids my age. We played ping-pong. My sister arrived, but not my mom.

My aunt (my dad's sister, who lived nearby) arrived at our house to be with my mom. The ambulance took my dad away. Kind neighbors reassured me he would be okay. And I felt like he would. I needed to see him, to hold him, to hug him, and be reassured that he was fine.

Not long after, my sister (who had been found in the closet by my aunt) and I piled in the back of my neighbor's car, and we were driven to the hospital where my dad was taken. We continued to be reassured that dad was okay. After all, how could he not be? He was my hero! An army colonel, ranger, and decorated war veteran, there was no one stronger or more resilient than my dad. If anyone could make it through this, it was him.

We arrived to the hospital and were swept to a private room with comforting colors and lighting. That was odd. Why are we in this room? I thought. Neighbors and family members gathered around my sister and me to comfort us. But still, my mom and aunt were missing.

What was going on? "Where is Dad?" I kept asking out loud and wondering to myself. A few moments later, my mom and aunt entered the room, and my life would be forever changed.

"Ashley and Alexandra," my mom said with quivering tears, "Daddy is in heaven."

What? I thought. How? My hero, my play buddy, my favorite person in the entire world. Gone. Just like . . . that?

Shock hit my sister and me like the biggest tidal wave. I couldn't grasp what was happening. I didn't even cry at first. I was angry. I was abandoned. My mom, sister, and I embraced each other and then collectively wept. I remember the entire room—us, my aunt, family members, neighbors—we all wept in shock.

Nothing we could do (or that the paramedics could do) could have saved him. The autopsy report stated that 90 percent of his heart was blocked. Yet, for years I lived with guilt that I didn't call 911 fast enough, that it was my fault that the medical help didn't arrive soon enough to save him.

DAILY AFFIRMATION

During the darkest days, when it's difficult to find the light and hope, repeat this mantra to yourself: "This is only temporary; this is only temporary."

I want to pause for a moment, dear reader, and tell you how hard it was for me to write the above account of my father's death. Even 26 years later, at 38 years old, writing about the tragic and sudden loss of my father triggered me to tears. After I finished writing the above, I had to stop. I closed my laptop. I felt a sudden wave of grief wash over me and I began sobbing. I texted my husband and asked him to come home from work. I reached out to a dear friend and told her what just happened. I'm writing this to say and show you first, how far I've come in even being able to verbalize and share my trauma, and my feelings. Eleven-year-old Ashley did not do this. High school Ashley did not do this. College Ashley didn't either. Nor did young mother Ashley. She did not talk about her grief, her trauma, and her loss.

Most damaging to my well-being, I spent years not wanting to speak with anyone about losing my father, despite multiple counselors and family members trying to help. I instead buried these feelings of sadness, guilt, and regret deep within. I wasn't doing, and didn't even attempt, the healing work I needed to do. I put on the "mask" of strength and went through the motions of life, wanting to feel loved, yet always feeling lost. On the outside, I looked like I had it all in high school. I was well liked among peers, a leader, a dancer, and I had a dream to become a news anchor one day. On the inside, I was lonely, sad, insecure, and had attempted to bury those messy feelings of grief and trauma because it seemed easier to do.

I continued numbing and ignoring negative thoughts, feelings, and experiences until I was thirty-three and the universe knocked me over the head with a second major traumatic event. I had been living what seemed to be my dream life in New York City. "Work hard, play hard" was my mantra, and I was the stereotypical overachieving, workaholic, partying professional. I spent long workdays as a producer for CBS News, and I traveled the country covering breaking news stories. Ironically, most of the stories I covered were very, very tragic. The Virginia Tech massacre.

Missing children. Mass shootings. Missing and murdered mothers. Instead of focusing on my own tragedy, I was wrapped up in covering others. It was the perfect gig to avoid focusing on "me," the little Ashley that was still carrying around the guilt and pain of her father's death.

I never took the time to really dive into what I was feeling, which was exhaustion, loneliness, lack of self-worth, regret, guilt, and more. I numbed myself with my newsroom career, ready to jump at the next breaking news story—the missing person, the mass shooting, the election. . . . You name it, I covered it. And when I wasn't working, I barely slept. Instead, I would get off a late shift and go to a bar to meet up with friends, only to return to work the next morning at 4:00 a.m. to get ready for our live show. I would often sleep on my boss's couch to avoid the commute to my apartment in Hoboken. Don't get me wrong, I was really good at my job and I was driven to be the best booking producer out there. And I was also really good at thinking and pretending to be okay, and I'm pretty sure I led people to believe I was.

After four years of working like a maniac at CBS News, I took a job in Washington, D.C., working for a new cable show that focused on energy and environmental issues, which I absolutely loved. My partying calmed down a bit, but I still hid from myself by diving into my work. I continued traveling the world covering breaking news stories. Somewhere in the middle of this madness, I developed a relationship with a wonderful man who saw enough in me to marry me. I thought I had achieved it all: the great TV journalism career, the happy marriage, and the three beautiful children that followed. But then, boom. Everything came crashing down.

In 2014, I became extremely sick with a mystery illness that left doctors stumped. At first, I thought it was a bad flu, or a stomach bug, because I couldn't keep any food down. By this time, I was in the process of launching my own media relations company, so I thought it might be the stress of being an entrepreneur for the first time. I started losing weight, suffering from malaise and brain fog, and seemed to become allergic to all of the food I was eating. Then I became pregnant with our third child and the symptoms mysteriously disappeared. I felt pretty good during those nine months of pregnancy.

But from the moment my sweet Scarlet was born in November 2015, the symptoms came back tenfold. I was barely functioning. I constantly felt like I was going to pass out. I was dizzy, had brain fog, my body was numb, I saw white flashing lights in my vision. I had severe nerve pain all over my body, no appetite, and so much more. Having just delivered my third child, doctors diagnosed me with severe postpartum depression, and I was committed to an outpatient psychiatric program and loaded up with psychiatric drugs. I was so sick with fatigue, flu-like symptoms, and mental psychosis that I could no longer care for my family. I wanted to die and felt like I was dying.

I had spent nearly a year and a half at this point visiting up to thirty different medical professionals—infectious disease doctors who told me I just had "anxiety" as a new mom, gastrointestinal specialists who told me I was just recovering from a "stomach bug," and internists telling me it was the postpartum depression. Chronic fatigue syndrome, fibromyalgia, IBS, I had been given every diagnosis possible. My mother-in-law suggested that I get "just one more opinion" from a highly recommended infectious disease doctor. And this was the miracle day, my first appointment with Dr. Marsha Soni. She listened to me cry, with my husband by my side, for nearly forty-five minutes. I'll never forget the words she spoke, which validated what I already suspected: "You have Lyme disease." She ran tests to confirm and began treating me through IV antibiotics.

During the period of healing after my visit with Dr. Soni, the concept of hope was similar to a roller coaster. One day I would feel a bit better and even possess the courage that I had a proper diagnosis, and I would find a glimmer of hope. The next day, I would feel terrible and couldn't get out of bed, and was filled with despair. I could not muster up a mask of strength at this point; I had no energy to even fake it.

Not only was my physical health failing during this time, but my mental health was, too. I was in despair and severely depressed. Finding hope in the middle of all this seemed like an impossible and even unworthy task. One of the blessings of my career as a publicist are the people I've connected with on TV sets, such as Malena Crawford, transformation coach and author of *A Fistful of Honey*, a novel of spiritual and emotional healing.

"Trauma drains us in many ways, making even the most mundane activities challenging, like getting out of bed," says Malena. Among the many healing techniques I learned from Malena is self-compassion. "Trauma is the time to wrap yourself up in compassion and give yourself the sacred space and time to heal."

I can attest to the power of self-compassion as a path to healing. I would have not recovered physically if I had not first taken care of myself emotionally and spiritually. The person I was before my health crisis— the highly stressed Type A perfectionist and people-pleasing party girl —is not the person I am today. My health crisis stopped me in my tracks, and just in the nick of time. All the stress in my body, coupled with holding in the trauma over the years, likely caused a release of the "fight-or-flight" hormone called cortisol. Too much cortisol is known to speed up the reproduction of the Lyme bacteria.

I can now call my health crisis "the gift of Lyme." It taught me how to prioritize my emotional and spiritual health to protect my physical health.

I believe in my heart of hearts that *hopeful practices result in positive transformation.*

Malena Crawford said it best: "You are not your trauma, but you can be powerfully and positively transformed by it if you are willing to. You are resilient and you will survive."

HEALING PRACTICE

Connect back to the creative things you loved to do as a child and start incorporating them into your day. Find activities you loved to do as a child and practice them a few times a week for a month. Journal what this experience is like for you. For me, this was dancing, singing, reading, and writing.

"BUT FEELINGS
CAN'T BE IGNORED,
NO MATTER HOW
UNJUST OR UNGRATEFUL
THEY SEEM."

–ANNE FRANK,
THE DIARY OF A YOUNG GIRL

CHAPTER 2

EMBRACE THE WAVES OF EMOTIONS

Emotions. They're messy, they're sometimes ugly, and they're just overall icky when you're dealing with a challenging issue or traumatic event. They can wash over you like a tsunami wave, and leave you feeling battered and bruised on the beach, and scrambling for a higher ground away from what seems like an emotional wreckage.

I avoided my emotions for years after my father's death, shoving them into dark corners of my mind, my heart, my body. Instead of doing the work of embracing my emotions, I instead escaped into my work as a network producer, keeping too busy to make time or space for my feelings. I believe deep in my soul that the emotional avoidance creates a deep and damaging internal stress that only exacerbates other issues, and in my case, Lyme disease.

"The greatest lesson anyone can learn is how to ride those waves of emotion instead of avoiding them," says Julie Reisler, author of *Get a PhD in YOU*, and faculty member at Georgetown University's coaching program. As my own coach, Julie threw me multiple lifelines as I rode the waves of emotions.

FEELING AFFIRMATION

Put your hands on your heart and ask yourself, "What am I feeling? What part of myself is hurting?" Then tell yourself it's okay to feel all of it.

What Julie helped me understand is that avoiding your emotions is like riding on an empty ship—you've literally abandoned yourself. That's when your health, your energy, and your hopeful self start to suffer. The way to end this abandonment is to access your heart and do practices that keep you there, as Julie so wisely taught me.

"We all know that the heart is an actual muscle in the body, but it is also a muscle of wisdom," explains Julie. Building up your heart wisdom starts by honoring and accepting your perspective and emotions. "Whether you are going through an individual trauma, or are feeling the collective trauma in the world, we are experiencing a massive shift in becoming more heart-centered as a human family," Julie says. "Let your heart go first, then your mind," Julie encourages. "Don't let your brain judge or berate your feelings. Trust the inner wisdom in your heart."

For me, the best way to still my hyperactive mind is through meditation. (More on that later.) It helps me calm down to do deeper emotional work that I can find so many reasons to avoid. I also make space and quiet time for journaling—the sacred act of writing where you can speak and reveal anything you need to share in the privacy of your own notebook. If you're like me, you probably grew up being told to be nice, don't get angry at anyone, or be anything less than always positive. Journaling is a safe space to wrestle with and release all those ugly and uncomfortable emotions.

"Once you ride your emotions for a while, then you can move on to the deeper work," Julie says. "It's like diving down farther into the ocean versus staying on the surface. Riding the waves on the surface helps teach us that it's safe to have feelings. And once you feel safe, you can start doing more of the deeper work."

I've learned that this bottom-of-the-ocean deep work is where the real breakthroughs happen. Some people call it shadow work, dealing with the parts of us that we want to hide or deny or have shame about. "If you don't go through the tunnel with the shadows, it's going to be hard to get to the other side," Julie says. "Once you start to uncover all that is happening, that healing wisdom in your heart starts to emerge. You begin to tap into your intuition and heart guide we all have within."

Finding that inner guide is what gives you true healing and strength.

I know that the inner heart guide gives you the ability to meet whatever you are feeling with compassion, and truly see and accept yourself instead of abandoning yourself. It's developing the practice of having a safe, nonjudgmental conversation with yourself: "What do you need? I'm here. How can I serve? How can I help you? I love you and I'm not leaving you."

Remember—there's wisdom and healing in those messy 'ol emotions.

HEALING PRACTICE

Set aside just one hour a week for "mental hygiene"—journal
all your feelings without judging or editing yourself.

_____

_____

_____

_____

_____

_____

_____

_____

_____

_____

_____

_____

_____

_____

_____

_____

_____

_____

_____

"WHEN YOU CHANGE THE
WAY YOU LOOK AT THINGS,
THE THINGS YOU
LOOK AT CHANGE."

–ESTHER HICKS,
AUTHOR OF *THE LAW OF ATTRACTION*

CHAPTER 3

GET PRIMAL WITH YOUR MELTDOWNS

If you're anything like me, you try to start the day with a bit of positivity and hope. That's why I love mornings. I love watching the sun rise, and I love writing in the morning. I try to meditate daily, though I definitely miss it on certain days. I breathe deeply when I am feeling anxious. I turn off the news when it is too much. But what I have learned over the years, and through the interviews I conducted for this book, is that not being okay is absolutely okay.

Has anyone ever told you to "cheer up"? Or, "You're strong, you can get through this"? I cringe when I hear those words. Even my husband has been guilty of saying this line to me, and it infuriates me. Why try to be happy when you simply aren't feeling happy? Why does society, and our friends and loved ones for that matter, encourage us to feel happy or strong when, in fact, we're not feeling either? Why is it when you ask a friend, "How are you doing?" the usual answer is, "I'm fine," when you know they really aren't?

I read an article in my local newspaper, the *Washington Post*, about "toxic positivity" and how it can cause more harm than good. And I think that is especially true for anyone experiencing trauma in their life, whether it's the death of a loved one, the loss of a business, fighting a chronic or life-threatening disease, or severe anxiety and depression.

What happens when you are so filled with emotions that you feel yourself literally shaking and have a primal urge to do something that feels destructive? Dr. Jamie Hope, emergency room physician in Detroit, explains that ignoring that primal part of who you are is not serving yourself, and, in fact, is denying who you are and your basic humanity.

"Stress is a natural reaction to a threat. For our ancestors, it served a very important purpose, like getting up the energy to run from a saber-tooth tiger, for example. It's the flight or fight hormone that protected our ancestors, but that same stress hormone today can be destructive to our emotional health. Most of us don't always make the time to run the stress hormone off."

Hope says that when she sees something terribly tragic at work, something awful that human beings do to each other, she doesn't feel so warm and fuzzy. "I get mad, and I have to release it. For some people, it's going for a run or taking it out on a punching bag or a pillow. People should have permission to take care of their primal urges to reduce stress and anxiety, but in a safe way."

One thing Dr. Hope suggests that can be incredibly satisfying is called dish therapy. "You get a cheap set of old garage sale dishes and smash them. You just let it all out. Here's a tip: break them into a metal trash can to make it even louder. Plus, you don't have to clean it up when you're done." (You may want to do this in a place where the neighbors won't see you.)

She emphasizes that this primal stress release needs to be done in a safe and controlled manner. "Number one, don't break anything that doesn't belong to you. And if you hurt yourself in the process and end up in the ER, that is not going to decrease your stress level."

Primal stress release is even necessary for kids. Dr. Hope uses soft fabric "angry dolls," her parental name for what are known as "dammit

FEELING AFFIRMATION

*I will release my feelings in a
safe way to achieve emotional
health and balance.*

dolls" among adults, which are used for everything from a favorite football team losing the big game to cancer patients facing painful treatment. "Instead of throwing tantrums, punching each other, and even biting, my kids have this constructive way to release these feelings instead of being told to squelch them."

She recommends having two stress-releasing tool kits. One is filled with soft things like dolls or pillows you can thump and whack. The other is filled with hard things like dishes to break or a stick to bang against a metal garbage bin. "If you can release stress in a safe way, it takes you out of a reactive mode and helps you to relax, think, be rational, and collaborate with your family, friends, and coworkers."

The most important thing I want you to know is that it is okay that you're not happy when your own world or the world around you seems to be falling apart. It is okay that you wake up sad, scared, and angry. You need to feel all of these feelings! I think this is an important process of life—to really feel what we are feeling—to talk about it and share it with others rather than sugarcoating it by posting happy pictures of #lifeisgreat and burying the feelings deep within. *Holding your feelings in never helps your emotional or physical well-being.*

What's better is sharing your feelings with someone who can help. I mostly navigate my household solo these days as my husband works very long hours, which leaves me caring for our three young children and running a company all at once. Recently, I had an especially hard day navigating virtual meet-and-greet with teachers and a few work hiccups, and it was just enough to put me over the edge. I felt the feelings bubble up and immediately called my mom on FaceTime. The moment I saw her, I burst into tears and let the river flow. She listened to me for an hour, and that primal release of feelings was all I needed to then take a deep breath and feel okay again.

HEALING PRACTICE

Take time to journal ideas to put together your own stress-releasing tool kits for the next time the universe throws you a curveball—don't forget to have both a soft and hard tool kit!

"FEAR IS LIKE A GIANT FOG.
IT SITS ON YOUR BRAIN AND
BLOCKS EVERYTHING–REAL
FEELINGS, TRUE HAPPINESS, REAL
JOY. THEY CAN'T GET THROUGH
THAT FOG. BUT YOU LIFT IT,
AND BUDDY, YOU'RE IN FOR
THE RIDE OF YOUR LIFE."

–BOB DIAMOND (ACTOR RIP TORN)
IN THE MOVIE *DEFENDING YOUR LIFE*

CHAPTER 4

LIFT THE
EMOTIONAL FOG

Messy, unaddressed emotions can feel very damaging and debilitating. I'm not talking about normal, short-term stress, such as waiting to sign a new client at work or worrying about your child passing their math finals. I'm talking about that excessive fear, worry, and despair that cause actual physical changes and render us unable to take care of ourselves and our family, or even get out of bed.

Probably my lowest, most despairing moment was at one doctor's appointment where I was feeling exceptionally sick and experiencing dizziness and heart palpitations. I had decided to see a holistic medicine doctor as visits to traditional ones weren't yielding any relief. The kind doctor laid me down when I said I felt like I was going to black out. The room was spinning. I couldn't see my mom, who took me to the appointment, or my doctor. Everything was going in circle after circle. I started crying. I then lost complete control of my bladder (which is still an embarrassing thing to admit).

The doctor immediately administered an IV of vitamins, which didn't help, and an energy healer came to sit with me and calm me down. I was crying hysterically. The doctors decided my condition was not improving, so they called an ambulance to take me to Sibley Memorial

Hospital in D.C. My mother thought I was going to die that day. My husband rushed to my bedside in the hospital. I continued to have zero control over my bowels (I was literally just peeing in a bucket on a bed) and was given medication to try to stop the dizziness. We left the hospital with no answers, and I felt completely defeated and, honestly, was ready to die.

My undiagnosed Lyme disease had made me so physically sick that I could barely eat, and I had lost so much weight that I was too weak to even take care of my three girls. The doctors sent me home loaded up on drugs, and once again, without any clear answers as to what was happening to my body. I was left alone in my house (my husband took the kids to his parents' house so the girls didn't have to witness their mother so sick). The next day, I tried to get out of bed and I collapsed on the floor, screaming out and crying to God, begging for help and healing. I wanted the pain to end and was reaching my limit on life.

I know that when things go so terribly wrong, when your life seems to be spiraling down into a dark abyss, it is so easy for despair to take over. All you can see on the horizon is a thick, dark fog. You lose all hope of getting through to the other side. Fear has taken a hold of you, and your mind is stuck in a constant and crazy-making loop of negativity.

That's when you need to take it one step at a time. I'm a huge fan of the hit Disney movie *Frozen*, and in *Frozen II*, Anna, one of the main characters, sings a song, "The Next Right Thing." And that's truly what you need to do when you are in crisis mode and have no capacity to do anything else. Just take it one step at a time, and do the next right thing. That's what I had to do.

What's worse is that our culture suppresses anything low, dark, and often, too deep, including death, even though it is all around us and woven into our lives. "Culturally we expect the highs, but we don't expect the lows. And so, when we get very low, we beat ourselves up about it and think of it as a deep problem with the core of who we are,"

FEELING AFFIRMATIONS

*I honor and acknowledge my ability
to slow down in order to listen to my
inner voice and knowing.*

explains Marci Moberg, a dear friend, intuitive coach, and healer whom I have worked with for years post–Lyme disease recovery. Like me, Marci also shared a Lyme disease diagnosis, and she deeply understood the physical, emotional, and spiritual pain that I was enduring. "Rather, when you have lows, compassionately see it as a sign that you're human and that you feel. Feeling is a good thing, it reminds us we are alive, and a natural part of our experience."

During the darkest days of my Lyme disease, Marci's guidance helped me shift from an endless pattern of despair and anxiety into an awareness of what these feelings were actually telling me. "When we are highly anxious and out of touch with what our feeling is trying to tell us, a kind of looping happens in our minds. This frantic mental energy can gain momentum and sweep us up until we can barely function," Marci explains.

I know, for me, the more I feel messy emotions like fear, anxiety, and hopelessness build up, the more I try to push them away or dig my heels in and try to control things. The renowned psychiatrist Dr. Suvrat Bhargave, author of *A Moment of Insight*, works with families and children who experience extreme anxiety, leaving them feeling overwhelmed, distraught, and empty. He explains that anxiety has us either ruminating about the past or being fearful about the future. "Anxious people often try to control variables they cannot. One of the biggest lessons the pandemic has taught us is that there are circumstances out of our control. That should be empowering, because it helps us focus on things that we can control," he says.

Marci's technique for stopping anxiety from spiraling faster and faster comes down to two simple words: "Slow down."

Marci suggests that your messy emotions are likely to be a messenger for something quite important that is going on inside that we need to listen to. "It's difficult to hear what is going on inside when you are frantically moving physically or when your mind is racing and multitasking all the time. When you slow down your body and mind during times of fear and anxiety, you will have more space to tap into the GPS of your heart. This is where you'll reconnect to your deepest and best self. We all carry the kernel of wisdom within our heart that tells us what needs to be attended to or healed. We just need to slow down and remember how to listen to that inner voice."

When I first heard Marci suggesting I slow down, I scoffed. How could I? I have a business to run, clients to make happy, employees to nurture, three children to parent, a relationship to maintain with my husband. I have no time to slow down! Through her patient guidance, she helped me realize that the world outside of us is always going to try and tell us what we should think, what we should do, what we should want. But those external forces don't know what's right for us. And when we get unbalanced and out of touch with our inner voice and heart whisperings, that's when those hidden feelings of grief, sadness, despair, guilt, and anxiety can build until it damages us physically, like with my Lyme disease.

"Shifting away from all those other messy feelings to making space for awareness requires prioritizing time to reconnect to ourselves," Marci explains. "I like to suggest we treat connection with ourselves as a basic need and part of our daily routine, like brushing our teeth. Over time with practice, we can start to get curious about what wounds we need to address that are underneath our feelings or what part[s] of ourselves are challenging to be with [and] we need to get to know."

HEALING PRACTICE

Develop the practice of meditation in the morning, even if it is as short as a few minutes. Get in touch with the sensations in your body and in your heart, and honor what your inner voice is telling you. Ask yourself, "Why is this coming up for me now? What are my body and mind trying to tell me?" When I first started meditating, I couldn't even meditate for longer than thirty seconds, so remember to give yourself grace if you are a beginner. Journal what the experience was like for you.

"STAYING IN CONVERSATION
WITH THE GREAT FORCES OF
LIFE AND DEATH MAKES OUR
TIME HERE MORE PRECIOUS."

—MARK NEPO,
AUTHOR OF *THE BOOK OF AWAKENING*

CHAPTER 5

MAKE SPACE FOR THE BRAVE CONVERSATIONS

I'm not going to pretend this is going to be an easy chapter for you to read. It wasn't an easy chapter for me to write. It's not about the loss of a job, a business, a relationship, or even your health for a bit. I'm not denying those are significant emotional traumas. It's about facing the death of a loved one, or even your own death. The feelings of guilt, pain, grief, and darkness surrounding death can cast big, dark shadows over your life for a long time.

"Our culture is extremely death phobic," explains Dr. Martha Calihan, integrative and family medicine practitioner at Five Stones Healing Center, and author of *A Death Lived*. Her memoir shares her husband's final illness and death and how that process helped her address some of the big questions about end-of-life care and conversations.

Death has been brought front and center more recently in society as we've witnessed the suffering and passing of millions of people around the world due to COVID-19. The rapid-strike nature of the virus prevented many families from having any conversations with loved ones before their deaths. Or even being physically present as the dying were isolated in the infectious disease units of hospitals or long-term-care facilities.

"Before all the medical advances to prolong life over the last fifty years, death was a normal part of life," Dr. Calihan says. "People died at home and it just was what was experienced. Everybody was familiar with it. Today, there are a lot of people who've never seen a dead person, or witnessed a death, and it's a very scary thing for them."

Losing a loved one has been in my life since age eleven, and the fear of dying was instilled in me at a young age due to losing my father. I recently applied for life insurance after waiting several years post–Lyme disease. My husband, being a prepared planner and forward-thinker on life, had been begging me for years to apply, but honestly, I was scared. I'm not sure why. Perhaps it was the fear of being denied, being told my life wasn't worth putting a price on in case something happened to me. Perhaps it was that I just didn't want to address my death in any way.

After going through the life insurance application process, the paper-work, and the medical exam and bloodwork, I received a letter in the mail several weeks later. I was denied. The letter stated that it was due to the "ongoing COVID-19 pandemic." However, this spun me down the rabbit hole of emotions, including how death is around us every day, and we are all ill-equipped to handle it. Buying life insurance and drafting a will is often what people consider preparing for death. But those are financial and legal transactions, not the emotional and spiri-tual aspect to dying. Having conversations about the end of life—yours or a loved one—is something that is given very little guidance or space in our culture.

I was so young when my father died that my mother's focus was on ensuring financial stability for our family. My father was prepared for death from an insurance perspective. He was an army colonel and a war veteran, so he had excellent death benefits, and his wish was that my mother could stop working and care for the kids if he died. We were fortunate that this was possible. My mother left her successful dance company and studio she owned to care for my sister and me. She worked hard to create new and fun memories for us such as trips to Disney World, beach vacations, and lots of time with our relatives, both visiting them and having them in our home and as neighbors—my uncle moved in right next door and helped raise us. But perhaps because my mother still has trauma over the death of her beloved husband, having a "courageous conversation" about her end-of-life plans is a work in progress and delicate subject that we are still learning how to navigate.

While my Lyme disease didn't prove to be fatal, I certainly had many days when I felt like I was dying. However, I didn't communicate to anyone about my end-of-life plans because I didn't know what I wanted it to look like. Plus, our culture teaches us that death is scary. This is a mistake, because death is a subject we should all be talking about, with ourselves and with our loved ones and each other. Instead of seeing death as spooky (like a Halloween movie or costume), we all need to see dying as a beautiful process that has the potential to bring families closer together on a spiritual and emotional level.

"If your family or friends or whomever you choose don't have a clue what your value system is, or what you're thinking about these end-of-life decisions, you are not living your best life to the end," Dr. Calihan says. "Death can be a beautiful thing and a spiritual process, if you are really open to embracing it. It doesn't mean it's not hard and sad, but it can be beautiful. You're surrounded by the people who love you, who are there to help you through that transition and express your values as you leave this world."

It saddens me greatly that my dad was not given the opportunity to have his family help him through his transition in a gentle, loving way. While I never had these types of conversations with my father, I find

FEELING AFFIRMATIONS

*I am open to having brave
conversations about both
life and death with my loved ones.*

myself having these conversations with my children. They ask about death and dying and I am open with them about it. They know they have a grandfather who passed away when I was young. We visit his grave and we talk about him, and see his death as an opportunity to talk about life and life beyond this earth.

My children have an opportunity to learn about my values and beliefs, and therefore can begin to construct their own in a healthy and meaningful way. Though I know I still have a way to go to step into that conversation with them, and with my husband, about what I want my end of life to look like.

My wish for you is that this chapter will further deepen the conversation around end-of-life, and that it will give you the courage to do so sooner rather than later. I'm still actively undoing my cultural dispositions of seeing death as scary and have started having early conversations with my family about what death is and what I want it to look like for me.

A critical component of Dr. Calihan's integrated medical practice is encouraging her patients to have conversations about their death plan, as part of helping people achieve true balance of mind, body, and spirit. "I find that most people really want to talk about their end-of-life situation, but don't know how to start the conversation." To help patients get started, Dr. Calihan talks through some scenarios and offers questions to guide the process.

"Sometimes it helps my patients if I start by sharing my own end-of-life wishes. For example, I share with them that even though I am a medical doctor, I would like to not have a medicalized death. I'd rather be at home. I would turn down treatment that wouldn't allow me to stay at home." Dr. Calihan emphasizes that her son knows what's important to her, and she trusts that he would support her decisions. "I also let my patients know that you can never say for sure how you'll feel or make final decisions until you're facing your final days."

It's so important to answer these questions and have your

conversations before your health situation or that of a loved one becomes too intense. You don't want to wait until your mind isn't totally clear, or you aren't functioning at your full capacity.

Thankfully, there are many resources to guide families in having end-of-life conversations, and I've listed some in the back of the book. Some tips I like include:

- Have a practice conversation first before the real one with loved ones.
- You don't have to cover all the topics in the first conversation.
- Your loved ones may disagree with you—be patient and listen to their perspective.
- Nothing you decide is permanent.

Questions that I asked myself as I thought about my own end-of-life plan:

- What does a good day look like to me even as I'm dying?
- What kind of physical, emotional, and spiritual help do I want?
- What matters most to me through the end of life?
- How much medical care do I want?
- Where do I prefer to be when I die?
- Where is a good place to have the conversation? (At the kitchen table, on a walk, elsewhere?)

You may be asking by now: What do sometimes messy, difficult, and uncomfortable conversations on death have to do with owning our authentic power? For me, these conversations have brought me closer to how I want to live every day. It focuses my intentions on practices that will help me heal from any difficulties I am facing or will face and the confidence that I can live a joyful and hopeful life. If there was any "gift" in my father's sudden death, which has taken me decades to absorb and learn, it's that we never know when our last breath will be taken. To quote Atul Gawande in his book *Being Mortal,* "Our ultimate goal, after all, is not a good death but a good life to the very end."

HEALING PRACTICE

Write a letter to someone close to you who has died. Write it in your
journal, or keep it someplace where you can refer to it again and again.
Maybe the letter is to a grandparent who lived a long life, or a high school
classmate who died tragically too young. Express to them how they lived a
good life, and what meaning they brought to yours.

"GRIEF DOES NOT CHANGE YOU.

IT REVEALS YOU."

−JOHN GREEN, *THE FAULT IN OUR STARS*

CHAPTER 6

LEAN INTO THE POWER OF GRIEF

The word *grief* tends to be associated primarily with the death of a loved one. But, in truth, the feelings of grief—deep sadness, the pain of letting go, the lack of joy—apply to many of the traumatic losses we experience in life. The loss can be the end of a relationship through divorce or a breakup. The job you loved, now ended, due to layoffs or a buyout package you took. A business shuttered after pouring years of hard work and resources into it. For me, I had also experienced the loss of my health, and I grieved for it daily.

The pandemic that started in March of 2020 created a communal grief where we mourned the loss of our "old lives"—hugging a friend to cheer her up, attending celebrations like a graduation or wedding, rooting for our children at their athletic events, or hearing our favorite music in concert. The nonstop media coverage of COVID's death toll and its devastating economic impact on businesses and families has contributed to overwhelming grief for our communities and countries around the world.

"Grief is hard to talk about, and it is certainly difficult for most people to express," says Edy Nathan, psychotherapist, grief recovery expert, and author of *It's Grief: The Dance of Self-Discovery Through Trauma and*

Loss. I couldn't agree more, knowing how I for years avoided facing my own grief over my father's death. I first met Edy through my work as a publicist, and worked with her on media training for her upcoming book. From the moment we met, I was drawn to Edy's calming, kind, and poised energy, and I learned so much from her about grief in our media training session.

"Grief impacts your body, mind, and soul in complex and intricate ways," Edy explains. "It can cause your soul to become unbalanced. But giving yourself permission to feel the pain of grief is part of the necessary growth. If you approach grief like a dance, where you weave in and out of the feelings you have about your losses, you can gain a deeper, more spiritual understanding of yourself."

Approaching grief like a dance is something that deeply resonated with me. Growing up a dancer in my young life, I understood the beautiful composition and complexity that grief contains when relating it to dance. We move through it, we feel it, we express it, we release it. And we go through this process again and again, and we continue to heal through all of it.

Edy believes grief is a powerful way to discover deep parts of your soul, and the soul is what will offer up the path to relief. "Instead of letting grief take you down, honor its presence and value its teachings, which can lead to the depth the soul craves for and sometimes demands."

For too long, I tried to push away my pain over my father's death, instead of accepting it as a very necessary part of my growth. I numbed myself, mostly with alcohol and unhealthy relationships with men, especially in my college years when the feelings began bubbling up more frequently. For nearly fifteen years after his death, I had only visited my father's grave at Arlington Cemetery twice, because I simply didn't want to face his death front and center. It was easier, I thought, to ignore it and attempt to move on in life. To be "so strong." Boy, was I wrong. There had been celebrations to honor my father's legacy after his death, such as a conference room dedicated to him at Ft. Belvoir's Center for Army Analysis and a one-year memorial anniversary at our local historic Catholic church. Beyond that, I had kept my emotional door shut when it came to talking about my dad. I think it was even harder for me than my mom and sister, because everyone deals with and processes grief differently.

When Lyme disease hit me on the head, death felt near, and I began to revisit losing my father in a way I had never done before. I began to really feel the emotions of his death—and I still do. The other day was the twenty-sixth anniversary of his death, and in the past, I would go through the day ignoring it, burying the trauma and memory of trying to save his life deep, deep within. But on this particular recent anniversary, I let it all out. I cried. I felt the emotions of loss. I relived the moment of trying to save his life. I meditated. I listened to music. I cried in the shower. I talked to my family, to my mom and sister. We talked about my dad's memory. We acknowledged how hard it is to miss someone every day, even twenty-six years later, but knowing how proud he would be of all of us. And that his memory lives within us and around us.

I had deep grief over my actual Lyme disease diagnosis as well. That I would never live another day of my life without worrying about triggering it. My body had nothing left to do but release this grief over my fragile health. I sobbed. I screamed. I got on my knees and prayed. There was no possible way to hold in or bury my feelings anymore, and in a very primal way, I was releasing it all. My soul learned that grief for anything is meant to be processed externally through crying, laughing, moving, punching, and hugging. Internally, I found relief through prayer, meditation, journaling, and breath work.

Grappling with individual grief is something that we all have to face on our own, and in our own way. We all have internal voices and pieces of memory about a person or a situation that aren't shared by others. "Grief requires that you face yourself alone, in your own time, and in

FEELING AFFIRMATION

I move with the ebb and flow
of grief and find peace in
the seasons of life.

your own way," Edy explains. That's because we all have intricate histories, personalities, and triggers at play in our response mechanism. Edy gives the analogy of a seven-layer cake to explain how we each respond to a trauma surrounding a loss. "If someone has had a variety of traumas as part of their past, those traumas add more layers to the cake. What feels like trauma to one may not feel like trauma to another. The layer cake of trauma is different for everyone."

For example, if someone has a history of anxiety that it is triggered by isolation, losing their spouse to cancer will have a different grief response than someone who does not struggle with anxiety. "How each of us responds to grief depends a great deal on our personality type, support team around us, and the tools we can access for self-soothing," Edy says.

There are cultures where periods of grief are expected to last weeks, months, even a year. Maybe you remember from history class that Queen Victoria of England went into seclusion for a decade after the death of her beloved husband, Albert, and wore black for the remaining forty years of her life. While that may be an extreme (and perhaps unhealthy) way of dealing with loss and grief, you cannot rely on others' advice on when and how you should move on. I was a young girl when my father died, so I didn't have a choice of having a grieving period and was sent back to school in only a week.

But now when I face a loss, I listen to my heart to know how long I need for healing and what I should do to move through the grief. I lost a friend during the pandemic, and this triggered the feeling of grief in losing my dad. Instead of burying it, I used the techniques that I knew worked for me in the past. I've learned to ride the roller coaster of grief, and I know that it is okay to feel yourself spiraling down to the bottom and not be afraid of it.

"Anticipating what may trigger feelings of sadness around loss, and developing coping strategies, is extremely helpful," Edy explains. "They are often simple activities like practicing gratitude, reaching out to your support network, going for a walk, journaling, or other positive actions." She notes that these activities may seem like common sense, but when you're in the throes of grief, knowing what's good for you and doing it can be a big gap to close.

Here are some of Edy's go-to coping activities for people moving through grief:

1. **PHYSICAL ACTIVITY.** It releases brain chemicals such as endorphins, which help boost our moods. Studies show that exercise over the long term helps more than medication or psychotherapy in treating anxiety and depression.

2. **SAY YOU CAN.** Your brain is one of your biggest allies, but also your biggest detractor. You can change the way it holds on to information, memories, and trauma. Shift your internal voice from "I am overwhelmed" to "I want to feel better."

3. **GET CREATIVE.** In whatever that means to you. This will also help shift the brain to a more positive state. Drawing, journaling, crafting, or playing music works. If you've lost your job, visualize what a new, more interesting one would look like.

4. **REACH OUT.** Even though each of us has to face our own "layer cake" of trauma and grief, you don't have to be alone while doing so. Reach out to a friend for coffee or a walk. Get professional help if you are struggling to gain balance in your life on your own. I go to therapy once a week and have been for years since being diagnosed with Lyme disease and postpartum depression. Being able to talk it out with a trained professional with an objective view has provided me with the tools I need to cope with life's adversities. I look forward to it every week!

During the throes of lyme disease, I kept my coping strategies on a piece of paper right on my fridge. My coping strategies will look different from yours, but some of mine include: light a candle, listen to Christmas music, watch a ballet, take a bath, call a friend, walk in nature.

"The tendency is for people to avoid, ignore, and deny the need for help. Healing comes in many forms," Edy says. "The first item to healing is to define what healing means to you. Healing is not about forgetting; it is learning to live with your trauma and accept your losses with peace. Finding gratitude, believing in forgiveness, and allowing for sadness to have room to live are all part of the healing process."

Take Edy's encouragement to "dance with your grief" literally, as in moving your body. Grief can burrow down in our bones and make us feel rigid in body and soul. I was trained as a dancer, so I fall back on movement like yoga to get in touch with myself and my feelings. Gardening, tai chi, or simply stretching is a way to release grief's grip on you and find peace and acceptance.

HEALING PRACTICE

When grief overwhelms us, we often don't know where to turn for release and healing. Put together your own list of coping techniques that have worked for you in the past, or the ones you like from this chapter. Then, transfer this list to a beautiful piece of paper and decorate it with images of flowers, animals, or other things that represent peace and calm to you.

FEEL IT
TO HEAL IT

"EMOTIONS CAN GET
IN THE WAY OR GET
YOU ON THE WAY."

–MAVIS MAZHURA,
AUTHOR OF *NAVIGATING THE RAPIDS
AND THE WAVES OF LIFE*

CHAPTER 7

THE F.E.E.L. FRAMEWORK

By now you've heard my story of how I spent a huge part of my life either avoiding my emotions or letting them get stuck in my body, which left me physically sick and mentally teetering.

In the coming chapters, you'll learn specific techniques I used to get on my path to healing. But if I had to sum up in one word how I healed my mind, body, and spirit, it would be FEEL!

There's an adage in the work world that you can "fake it until you make it." That saying just doesn't work when it comes to emotional well-being. You can't fake your feelings by putting on a tough external demeanor or plastering a big smile on your face. It's not normal to be strong all the time and repress those messy and difficult emotions.

If you want to access your true, authentic power, it truly does start with giving yourself permission to feel. Invite those feelings to sit with you for a while, greet them as a friend with some wise knowledge for you, and listen carefully to what they are telling you. When you feel it, you heal it, and that is what will release the true, authentic you.

The narrative we often hear from society is that releasing your emotions is a sign of weakness. That is just not true. Emergency room physician Dr. Hope (remember the smashing dish therapy from

Chapter 3?) looks at managing her emotional well-being as visualizing a table filled with your hopes, your dreams, your family, your loved ones, your hobbies—everything is on this table. And that table is supported by four legs: nourishing food, energizing exercise, restorative sleep, and emotional stress release. "I look at those four legs, and make sure that I'm taking care of all of them, especially releasing the emotions around stress," Dr. Hope says. "People like to tell the world they are fine, but then a tension headache comes up, or your jaw is always clenched, or you're nauseated." We can't stop stressful emotions from coming into our life, but we can control how much we release them back out.

I came up with a F.E.E.L. Framework that guides me in dealing with all the emotions I encounter daily—from frustration at my kids when they get into squabbles with each other, to the stress of launching a new campaign for a client, to my feelings of imposter syndrome (writing this book was a big one for me!), and even unworthiness. And we all experience "off" days. The other day I woke up in a crummy mood and could feel depressive thoughts enter my mind. Instead of pushing them back down, I invited those messy feelings in with open arms.

As meditation expert Sarah Blondin describes, entering our emotions helps us become owners of our experience and to not be afraid or fearful to release these emotions. "These feelings mean you are human, alive, and everything we experience is passing by if you allow it. Don't resist it, Sarah teaches in her course, "This Deepest Self," which is available on one of my favorite meditation apps, Insight Timer.

The next time you're feeling a "messy" emotion bubble up, don't push it back down. I want you to welcome it in and use my F.E.E.L. Framework to help you move through it.

The F.E.E.L. Framework can be an internal dialogue, a meditation, or a writing practice that you can do practically anywhere. It's about reestablishing a connection with yourself, and your soul, and learning to become present in front of these experiences and emotions. It allows you to take a pause and get curious about what you're feeling. It can take you two minutes to do, or 30 minutes to do—that is up to you. But at the end of the F.E.E.L. process, you'll have spent some time tapping into your own authentic power by feeling through your emotions.

THE F.E.E.L. FRAMEWORK

F: Focus on your feelings and identify what it is you may be feeling. Give it a name. If you're unsure of how you are feeling, acknowledge that, too.

E: Enter within the emotion. Just as a hurricane has an eye of a storm, go to the center of that feeling by meditating on it and breathing through it.

E: Experience the emotion and become the owner of it. This might be uncomfortable, and that is okay. Breathe through it, sit with it, feel it, cry with it, laugh with it.

L: Learn from that emotion and listen to what it is telling you. There is a reason this emotion is coming up for you, so let it teach you!

Then, love that emotion back and thank it for moving through you. If you can be open to positive emotions like love and joy, you can be open to any emotions that you are feeling and see them as an opportunity to listen and learn from them.

I love to practice my F.E.E.L. Framework whenever I'm aware of an unpleasant emotion in my body. For example, as a business owner and leader, I often need to have difficult conversations with people that make me feel a bit nervous and anxious leading up to them. Will I say the right things? Did I do something wrong? What if I hurt someone's feelings or make them upset? These are just a few questions that start to loop around my very active, hypersensitive mind.

That's when the F.E.E.L. Framework comes in to help you move through your emotions, thoughts, and feelings.

First, **FOCUS** on your emotions. This is the first step to processing and moving through your feelings. Identify that feeling. Name it. And if you're not sure, ask yourself what it is you're feeling. If you are meditating through this, put one hand on your heart and take a deep breath and listen.

Next, **ENTER** into the emotion! That's right. I want you to walk straight into the emotion as if you were walking into the eye of a storm. This can be done through meditation, where you close your eyes and visually watch yourself enter into the word "anxious" or "nervous" or whatever you may be feeling. The point is to meet that feeling face-to-face.

Then, allow yourself to **EXPERIENCE** the emotion. This can be uncomfortable and is why we often want to avoid feeling messy emotions! Take a few deep breaths. Now knowing the emotion and having entered it, give yourself permission to feel it! Sit in quiet meditation and contemplation for several minutes focusing on the emotion. You can also journal your feelings and experience. And by journaling, I mean free writing—whatever comes to mind without worrying what you're saying or editing yourself.

Finally, listen to the emotion and use it as an opportunity to **LEARN** from it. You can even ask the emotion: "Anxiety, what are you here to teach me today?" Listen back for an answer.

After you go through F.E.E.L., I encourage you to lean into the feeling by writing about it, talking to a loved one or friend about it, or discussing it with a therapist. Let it be a safe and loving conversation with someone you trust if you are open to it.

FEELING AFFIRMATION

*I embrace and love all of my feelings
with gentle care and grace.*

If you want to journal this privately, the conversation can look something like this:

FOCUS on the feeling:
"I'm feeling sad today because I had a tough conversation with a client at work."

ENTER into the feeling:
"My client wasn't happy with our progress and it was hard for me to hear her frustration. Though I listened and shared my thoughts, I feel sad that I let her down. This emotion feels uncomfortable for me."

EXPERIENCE the emotion:
You can speak to the emotion by meditating on it with your eyes closed, moving through it via breath work, yoga, or a meditative walk, or even writing what you are experiencing. "Sadness, I see you, and I am feeling with you. It's okay to feel sad over this situation. I work hard and want all of my clients to be happy, but I know it's not possible to keep everyone happy. Sadness, I'm acknowledging you with my heart and offering up my love to you. I see you are here, and I'm sitting with you." Perhaps you feel physical discomfort. Notice where in your body you are feeling it. Is it your head? Your gut? Your shoulders? Your chest? Become aware of any physical sensations that come up when you are experiencing the emotion. Depending on how you are feeling, allow yourself to cry, scream, laugh, and physically experience the emotion, if you feel like it!

Finally, LEARN from the emotion by listening within and loving it back.

The conversation with the emotion can look something like this:

"Sadness, what are you here to teach me?" Get quiet and listen. Use this as an opportunity to have the emotion teach you something you need to know.

Then, love that emotion back. Bless it!

"This feeling of sadness will not last forever, and by acknowledging it I am therefore accessing the power within me to move through it. I love you, Sadness. Thank you for being here!"

After following the F.E.E.L. Framework, see where that feeling sits with you. It's very likely still there, but perhaps in a more gentle and loving way. You may find that you've begun to move through it. You may even feel a bit better! You may even feel like picking up the phone and calling a friend and verbally sharing how you are feeling. Journal more about the feeling and let the free writing flow!

The F.E.E.L. Framework can take as long or as short an amount of time as you like. It's an opportunity to pause and acknowledge how you are feeling in a loving and gentle way instead of blocking it and pushing it back down inside you. By practicing the F.E.E.L. Framework, my hope is that you find that you have so much power within you to move through messy emotions and feelings!

USING THE F.E.E.L. FRAMEWORK AS AN ACT OF SELF-KINDNESS

F.E.E.L. can be seen as a practice of self-kindness, which shouldn't be mistaken for self-care. "There's a difference between self-care and self-kindness," explains Dr. Jamil Zaki, professor of psychology at Stanford University and author of *The War for Kindness*. "Self-care is really removing yourself from the things that are upsetting you, while self-kindness is often embracing and focusing on the fact that one is suffering, not shying away from it, but leaning into it," he explains. Suffering is not something to be ashamed of, and in fact, "it's one of the things that connects us with everyone." It's okay not to be at our best, not feel our best, not do our best. "Have empathy for yourself, and others, too, who are suffering," he says.

EMBRACING SHADOW EMOTIONS

As a mom to three young kids, I experience a wide variety of emotions daily. Frustration, anger, joy, elation, wonder, fear, guilt . . . you name it. Kids somehow magically bring out every emotion in me. The good, the bad, and the very ugly, especially while dealing with postpartum depression after the birth of my third child.

My dear friend Dr. Claire Nicogossian, a clinical psychologist, clinical assistant professor, and author of *Mama, You Are Enough: How to Create Calm, Joy, and Confidence Within the Chaos of Motherhood*, addresses these ugly emotions we experience as parents and calls them "shadow emotions."

"I'm the worst mom ever!"
"I'm failing my children."
"I work so much, I'm neglecting my kids—I feel so much guilt!"

These are some phrases I've said both to myself and to my friends and family. I'm sure my kids have even heard me say these phrases, too. As a clinical psychologist, Dr. Nicogossian has spent twenty years hearing similar comments in her therapy room supporting mothers like me.

Dr. Nicogossian says that the words we use to describe ourselves matter.

"Words are the foundation of expression—opening a window, revealing our inner values, beliefs, thoughts, and how we see the world. And the words we use in mothering, not only with our children but with ourselves, are incredibly powerful."

When Dr. Nicogossian became a mother to premature twin girls, she learned early on that sharing her raw and honest feelings in those first years was often met with discomfort, or changing the subject, or encouraging her to focus on the positive. Which is similar to the feeling of needing to be strong on the outside, when you may be crumbling on the inside. "There seemed to be an unspoken taboo in motherhood—*don't talk about or share the challenging parts of mothering; keep those feelings to yourself*," she describes.

She says that by not being more open about shadow emotions, mothers can feel unequipped, isolated, and overwhelmed with their emotions, doubting their skills, abilities, and competency to be good at mothering.

"We all experience shadow emotions and shadow moments throughout motherhood. And in these shadow experiences, you're developing the wisdom, which many of us learn through experience, that motherhood is a very emotional journey, and we are not defined by shadow emotions, nor do we have to act on them."

Instead of being afraid of or judging ourselves for experiencing shadow emotions, Dr. Nicogossian wants moms to embrace and prepare for the emotions that will be experienced throughout motherhood. "Shadow emotions are part of the landscape of motherhood, sometimes like sitting on the beach watching waves come to shore, other times like rocky terrain, and sometimes like driving through fog. But whatever the shadow emotion experienced is, in motherhood, it creates a chance to learn about yourself, grow, heal. Shadow emotions don't have to dim the happiness and joy in motherhood; instead, what they can do is show us the places we need to take more care of in our emotional health."

Dr. Nicogossian says that in order to move through these "shadow emotions," we should embrace the sadness we feel and find self-compassion.

We all let emotions get stuck in our hearts and minds. The F.E.E.L. Framework helps you get these feelings out of the way, so you can get on your way to releasing the natural beauty and power within you.

Practice the F.E.E.L. Framework the next time you feel a messy emotion bubble up. Pause and take the time to process the feelings, and then journal what the experience was like for you. What did you learn from this experience?

"SOMETIMES HEALING LOOKS
A LOT LIKE SITTING STILL,
LYING DOWN, NOT SPEAKING,
NOT MOVING, AND NOT BEING
ABLE TO PROCESS ANYTHING
OTHER THAN THE WEIGHT
OF THE UNIVERSE PRESSING
INTO YOUR CHEST. DON'T RUSH
THAT TIME; THOSE FEELINGS
ARE IMPORTANT."

–TOPHER KEARBY,
BESTSELLING WRITER AND ARTIST

CHAPTER 8

THE INSIDE AND OUTSIDE OF EMOTIONS

The controlling boss. The angry neighbor. The snarly customer service representative. The cranky spouse. Friends who border on being hypochondriacs (like me!). Our first reaction to these types of people is probably to get annoyed by their behavior. Have you ever considered that these reactions are a result of emotions deep inside that haven't been dealt with yet?

I spent years avoiding the emotions buried deep inside me. I was fearful of facing my inner feelings, so I just kept running and running, here, there, and everywhere, eventually making myself physically sick and getting annoyed at everyone else.

"It's the running from what we feel that puts us in all these negative and unhealthy situations," explains trauma coach Dr. Sekuleo Gathers. For example, he notes that the reason the divorce rate is so high is that people have a difficult time being open, transparent, sensitive, and engaged with their partner in conversation. "You can't have real, true intimacy with someone if you're not intimate with yourself."

A lot of people were so uncomfortable with the quarantine period during the recent pandemic (beyond the pain of not seeing family and friends) because there was so much time to really sit with oneself. Being stuck at home means people couldn't run very far from their inner feelings. One of the silver linings of the pandemic is that it did serve as a time to uncover what's going on inside and how you want to live your life moving forward.

Annelies Richmond, breath work expert and director at SKY Campus Happiness Program, a program that offers breathing workshops to college students around the country, says that one of the challenges people face in going inward to their heart level is that their mind is always focused on the next thing. "Our minds have this crazy tendency to always jump to the next thing to find happiness. You think you're going to be happy when you get the perfect job, and you get the perfect job and the mind jumps again." She notes that over the last few decades, humans have been racing down the slope of being distracted by outward stimulation. Goldfish now have longer attention spans than most humans!

I'm not going to pretend that going inward doesn't feel lonely sometimes. As Anneleis explains, "The loneliness is trying to instruct us to go somewhere a little deeper, like you're wading into a pond. And if we dive a little bit deeper into that pond, we can connect to the source of joy and happiness. When you start to connect with yourself like that, all the outward things become better because you've experienced it inwardly."

Despite my business success and being blessed with a beautiful family, I still struggle with issues of self-worth. One of my go-to techniques for going inward is SKY Breath Meditation. It's a different way of meditating; Dr. Emma Seppälä says that it immediately taps into the opposite of your fight-or-flight response. She explains that the sympathetic nervous system triggers the fight-or-flight response, whereas the parasympathetic nervous system controls the rest-and-digest response. By using breath work, you're able to tap into your parasympathetic nervous system,

FEELING AFFIRMATION

*The gift of breath is a reminder
that I have constant access to
calm, peace, and clarity.*

calming your heart rate and lowering your blood pressure in minutes, according to Dr. Seppälä.

"You can notice an immediate effect. This is a very efficient and effective way to come to a meditative state," she says. "You're actively changing your breath during SKY Breath Meditation, and it's bringing you into this deep state of relaxation that has these impacts on your mental health and well-being."

"Breath work actually helps you circumvent your mind. It doesn't let you talk yourself out of emotion," explains Anneleis. There's an actual physiological benefit that happens with breath exercises in that they activate the vagus nerve, the main nerve that sends messages to all the other nerves. When that nerve is stimulated, all kinds of wonderful things happen in your body, including changing your mood and creating a healthy immune system. The FDA is even testing how stimulating the vagus nerve can help treat severe cases of depression.

Breath work is so powerful in releasing messy emotions, as I learned during a virtual retreat with my friend Kushal Choksi, a former financial executive, and now an entrepreneur and practitioner of the SKY Breath Meditation. "One thing I always ignored was myself. Family, work, friends, everything was ahead of myself. I was never on the priority list. You have to dive in deeper and see for yourself how, you know, how things are playing out for you."

Kushal noticed that, every once in a while, a voice would come up from inside that said, "Hey, don't ignore me. Look at me; smile at me." So many distractions were around him, so many responsibilities, that emotions kept being put under the carpet all the time.

"Nobody has taught us how to tap into that inner dimension. You're always distracted. We all need tools to go inwards, then there's no way the emotions or the anxieties or the thoughts that are troubling can take over you. And that gives you so much strength when you tap into that inner dimension, and then you feel like it's going to be okay."

What I learned from Kushal is that every emotion has a specific breathing pattern. Think about it—when you're happy, your inhalation is slower. When you are stressed, your exhalation is stronger. Your breath is a barometer for how you're feeling. Controlling your breath can help you manage your mind and emotions.

Breathing is one of the simplest techniques we can do to process our feelings and stabilize our emotions. Breath work brings us back to the present moment. Here is a simple breath exercise to get started:

- Take a moment and put your hand on your belly.
- Breathe in through your nose for four seconds, hold your breath for five seconds, and release out for eight seconds.
- Repeat this a few more times. Feel your belly lift up and down as you breathe in and out.
- Notice how you feel. Getting into the present moment through breath work is one of my most powerful ways to access the healing within me, and it can be for you, too.

Jon Paul Cremini is another leading breath work practitioner, and his technique has quickly become one of my favorite ways to focus on my breath to get into my feelings and be in the present moment. Here's his approach:

- Lie down on the ground.
- Breathe in through your mouth using your belly.
- Breathe in again in your chest, and then breathe out fully.

His live classes, which he offers every Sunday (both online and in person), guide participants through thirty minutes of breath work, followed by the primal screams, which is such a powerful and profound combination!

We often forget to breathe. Do you notice that when you are nervous or stressed, you hold your breath? When we are anxious, we breathe faster. If you find yourself feeling anxious, stressed, worried, or low, focusing on your breath can be one of the most powerful ways to access your inner power. It can stop you in your cycle of emotions and bring you immediately back to the present moment. I practice breath work everywhere. In the car, on a walk, and even as I write this sentence. I notice my belly moving up and down. I listen to my breath release into the air. I hear the sound of air enter my nostrils. Breath work to me is like exercise for my soul. In the same way we work our physical bodies through running, dancing, and weight lifting, we have an opportunity (and in my opinion, a need) to access our breath to keep our souls fit.

"Breath work is a powerful science of its own that calms your physiology, and then the mind gets calm as a result. And you're not struggling to make the mind quiet. The mind effortlessly becomes quiet and calm, but also focused and alert," Anneleis often reminds me.

So, after my breath work or my meditation, I'm feeling pretty heart-centered, right? Then I start going about my day, and I feel that centeredness slipping away. One of the reasons for me is that I'm an empath—someone who is highly sensitive to the emotions of those around them. I'm so in tune with others' feelings, in fact, that, like a sponge, I start taking on their feelings myself. That's all fine when the people around you are happy and positive. But if someone is angry at me (like my girls when I cut off their TV viewing) or someone close to me is very upset (my husband about a work issue), I can feel myself getting tangled up in all these messy emotions. This leaves me feeling overwhelmed and exhausted and totally out of balance.

We can always return to a place of balance and focus simply by returning to our breath.

Ahhhh . . . what wonderful feelings can emerge to the surface using this tool that is with us all every second of every day.

HEALING PRACTICE

Begin developing your breath work practice by taking ten deep breaths every morning when you wake up and are still lying in bed. This helps you set your breath awareness for the remainder of the day. Journal what you noticed in your mind and body after you complete the breathing exercise.

"HEALING YOURSELF
IS CONNECTED WITH
HEALING OTHERS."

–YOKO ONO

CHAPTER 9

CONNECTING FOR HEALING

Most people's reaction to a trauma is to shut down, on themselves and on the loved ones in their life. I shut down feelings about my father's death for decades. When I was diagnosed with Lyme disease, I was so overwhelmed with anxiety and fear for my health and that I wouldn't be there for my husband and children—maybe forever. I'm also a people pleaser, and I hate confrontation, and so I often would go into my shell and hope it would all just go away.

"It's not a good idea to lock yourself away in your house because the loneliness, depression, and deprivation of joyful activities will generate a lot of stress," says Dr. Habib Sadeghi, founder of the Be Hive of Healing Integrative Medical Center and author of *The Clarity Cleanse: 12 Steps to Finding Renewed Energy, Spiritual Fulfillment, and Emotional Healing*. "Research has shown that stress absolutely suppresses the immune system and makes us more vulnerable to everything from colds to cancer. So fear-based self-isolation is the worst thing you could do for your mind, body, and spirit," he explains.

Researchers from Massachusetts General Hospital (MGH) published a study in the *American Journal of Psychiatry* naming social connection as the strongest protective factor for depression. And yet social connection can seem like the absolute hardest thing to do when you are feeling depressed and lonely. When I was in the depths of my postpartum depression and Lyme disease, it was so hard to muster up strength and courage to try to "connect" with someone, including members of my own family. Yet whenever I did, I found it helped in many positive ways.

During the pandemic, the intense feelings of unpredictability, uncertainty, and quarantining created tremendous stress on people. We all struggled to find ways to sustain our personal connections through technology. On one hand, I'm grateful we had our basket of technology tools to check in on family members, celebrate birthdays and graduations, and schedule weekly "venting" calls with friends about this once-in-a-life experience that upended everything we knew as normal. It was very hard to stay positive during those dark days when a vaccine and the reopening of the economy seemed so far away.

"Without social interaction, it's easy for people to collapse emotionally and fall into hopelessness. We know the rate of suicides, attempted suicides, and depression increased at an alarming pace as the shutdown dragged on," said Dr. Sadeghi.

Dr. Anisha Abraham, faculty member at Georgetown University Hospital and author of *Raising Global Teens: A Practical Handbook for Parenting in the 21st Century*, notes that "when you have any kind of transition or change, much less when you're going through a pandemic, it's those connections and having that community that are so important. Being able to share feelings is a way of staying stronger, and helps handle all the uncertainty around you."

My journalism DNA kicked into gear during the pandemic, and I started to research the experts who understand how to stay positive in challenging times. My research led to the Science of Well-Being course offered online through Yale University, led by Dr. Laurie Santos, a psychology professor at the school, and host of the popular podcast *The Happiness Lab*. I signed up immediately.

FEELING AFFIRMATION

I honor my own authentic power
by first connecting to myself,
and then to others.

One of the things that Dr. Santos could not emphasize enough is that social connection is what makes us more likely to survive illness, whereas the lack of it makes us susceptible to fall prey to life circumstances and experience premature death. She explained that people underestimate the importance of social connections and talking to people, and that many think they can be happy in solitude, especially with all the media options to keep our minds preoccupied. (How many shows did you binge-watch during the shutdown?)

I'm a natural born connector in many ways, especially in my work where I introduce clients to media opportunities and build meaningful relationships with members of the press. I do get energy from other people. Some even call me a social butterfly! But I can morph into an introvert when it comes to sharing vulnerable feelings. It takes a lot of courage to share how we are really feeling. Society can be so judgmental on people who open up.

In the darkest moments of my Lyme disease, when I felt like I was dying every day, I emailed my strong group of high school friends, whom I lean on when times get tough. I totally opened up with them, sharing my deepest fears and asking for their prayers and support. They met me with love, grace, and compassion through visits, phone calls, and texts.

Somehow, in the middle of my Lyme disease battle, when I couldn't dance or do any physical movement, I joined my church choir. I found the connections and friendships that come with making music so therapeutic. I also joined a Lyme disease support group for a short time, but I found the group had a "victim mindset," which I couldn't relate to. It's okay to try different connections and give yourself permission not to choose the ones that don't work for you.

"The worst thing to be when you're nervous or scared is alone. Humans are social creatures, and we need mutual interaction to be happy and healthy. Joyful human interaction and physical touch are as important to our health as anything we put in our mouths," says Dr. Sadeghi.

My tendency to head for my turtle shell to avoid uncomfortable feelings has caused at various times real tension with my husband. In the heat of a disagreement or misunderstanding, I can't always process my feelings in a healthy and productive way. So I call a "time-out" and take some time to write my feelings down and get to know them better. Then I can share my feelings more clearly with my husband. This approach has resulted in some very beautiful conversations and a deeper connection between us.

My dear friends Chris Winfield and Jen Gottlieb, who are both business and life partners, are known as "superconnectors" in their fields of coaching and media. They believe that people who make authentic and generous connections are more successful personally and professionally. In fact, they even named their company Superconnector Media.

"To really connect, you have to first reconnect to the best parts of yourself," explains Chris. "Then you can put those best parts out into the world." Sometimes, though, explains Jen, connecting to the best part of yourself is difficult, as we tend to see ourselves through a cloudy lens of self-doubt or harsh judgment. "I was listening to a friend tell me how much of an imposter she felt like. And I suggested she change the conversation with herself, and focus on all the amazing things that she had done in her life," says Jen.

She started an exercise called "the badass list," where she encourages people to write down all the times in their lives when they've done something really strong or admirable. You then hang the list on the wall and look at it every time you feel nervous or not worthy or disconnected from people. "It could be something as big as when you gave your first big presentation on a stage, or when your child said they loved you for the first time," Jen explains. "Whenever you're not feeling good enough to do something, read that list out loud."

This badass list has helped me get the courage to have those difficult emotional conversations with clients, employees, friends, my husband, my mom, my sister, and children.

Another amazing connecting tool Chris invented is called H.O.P.E.—Helping One Person Every day. Being of service to others helps you get your head out of your own problems, and creates a meaningful connection with someone else that turns out to be healing for you. The H.O.P.E. Framework works for anyone in your life—business colleagues, friends, and family. Instead of asking people, "How are you?" start the conversation with "What can I help you with today?"

For example, I started a book club in the summer of 2020 after the riots around the country following the George Floyd murder. I took a chance and reached out to the author Jayne Allen, whose book *Black Girls Must Die Exhausted* we were reading, and asked if she would be willing to participate in our discussion via Zoom. To my surprise, she said yes! After the discussion, I asked her, "What can I help you with?" She expressed her dreams to work with a large publisher. Through my contacts in the media and publishing world, I was able to connect her to the right people who helped her land a four-book deal at HarperCollins.

This notion of "what can I do to help" is similar to the random acts of kindness philosophy. One of the key points Dr. Santos made in the Science of Well-Being class is that there is a strong correlation between kindness and happiness. An easy thing you can do is show kindness to anyone you meet during the day—make an authentic connection with a stranger at the grocery store, the drugstore, in your yoga class, anywhere. Ask them questions like, "How are you doing?" or "What's your favorite snack?" or compliment them on their shirt or smile. Remember the "pay it forward" movement of a few years back, when a stranger in front of you at the coffee shop would pay for your drink? Dr. Santos reminds us that these random acts of kindness can create a social connection that elevates our happiness quotient. Not every feeling we share with others needs to be "messy"—a simple "thank you for being you" can go a long way. If there is a silver lining to the pandemic, it's the realization we've all had on how much we need human connection.

HELPING YOUR KIDS BUILD MEANINGFUL CONNECTIONS

Helping your children foster meaningful connections is one of the most important jobs we have as parents. Creating strong connections will give them a powerful tool to overcome difficult times. Dr. Abraham says that "being able to handle life's challenges is the biggest predictor of success in life. Teach your children to know how to handle the unpredictable moments, and get back up on your feet when things get tough."

My parents' generation (the Boomers) were taught to suppress their feelings, and that societal attitude filtered down into how they did (or didn't) teach me to express my emotions. It's not a criticism; it's a generational difference. Today, we are more culturally aware of the importance of talking to our children about their feelings.

Modeling to our children how to handle setbacks and disappointments through sharing feelings is so critical. We do our children a disservice when we don't show our own struggles or disappointments. We don't want to scare them or make them overly worried about their parents, but there are ways to use emotional conversations as teaching moments.

Children are naturally created with "no filters" when it comes to expressing their observations or feelings. How many times have you laughed (or cringed) when your child blurted out a rather direct comment in public about someone's appearance or behavior? There's a lesson for us adults and parents in connecting to our primal feelings.

But not all children know how to express what they are feeling. That's why you sometimes see "feeling charts" in a doctor's or therapist's office. They typically have pictures of little characters expressing anger, fear, sadness, and other emotions. I recommend a feeling chart for your home to help your child find a way to express themselves. We have one on our fridge and my kids use it often, especially when they can't find the right words to express how they are feeling.

FEELING AFFIRMATION

*I am a happier and healthier
person when I connect to myself,
and then to others.*

My healing would have not happened without the dozens of connections I made, many of whom are featured in this book. By creating a safe space for me to share my feelings, and through their act of honoring them, I have emerged a more courageous communicator and stronger human being and am able to model it for my children as well.

CONNECTING WITH NATURE

In the years before my dad died, I grew up with a beautiful pond in my backyard in a suburb outside Washington, D.C., that was perfect for fishing, bike riding around, and taking leisurely walks with my family. I even remember the time my dad let me "ice skate" on the pond once it had been frozen for weeks during a very cold winter. As a child, I would spend my days biking around my neighborhood, often alone, soaking in the fresh air while surrounded by beautiful trees. I'd come home for dinner, only to rush back outside to play "kick the can" with the neighbors through dusk. Nature was how I connected with myself and my spirit, yet somehow, after my father died, I lost my connection with it. In my high school, college, and journalism years, I was much more focused on pleasing people, being well-liked, and working my tail off to get ahead in the newsroom. Never mind the fact that I didn't pay daily attention to my gorgeous commute from Hoboken, New Jersey, to New York City, which provided breathtaking views of the Hudson River and the skyscrapers. Houseplants? I didn't even have one to try to kill if I wanted to (I have a love-hate relationship with my houseplants). I had lost connection with myself by losing connection with nature.

When Lyme disease hit me and I was forced to my bed, I remember wishing and wanting to be outside in nature. My soul craved connection with the outdoors—with the grass, the birds, the dirt, the sunshine. I would often close my eyes while suffering from physical pain, and imagine being at a beach. In my early meditations, I took myself somewhere outside my pain, and into beautiful forests with trees as tall as buildings, gorgeous ocean waves splashing at my feet, or hiking a dirt path on a mountain with breathtaking views.

As I began to very slowly feel better, I would take short walks outdoors. First, it was around the block on our street. Yet that small dose of sunshine, nature, and air, and communing with the elements, allowed me to connect back to my authentic self. It was as if my soul was remembering who it was. As the physical healing continued to happen and I was spending less time in bed, the more I craved being outdoors in nature. My husband and I would take the kids to visit local and state parks, visit new playgrounds, and walk around the local lake.

About two years into my Lyme recovery, several things happened that I can only contribute to divine timing and orchestration, which made my relationship with Mother Earth even more powerful. First, we moved into our "forever home," a beautiful plot of land with history that dates back to the Civil War. On our property, you'll find the oldest sweet gum tree in the state of Virginia (it is on the historic tree registry!), a vegetable garden, a quarter-mile long private driveway surrounded by luscious trees, a "wishing well," and a bamboo forest that my girls and I have dubbed "the enchanted forest." I have been blessed to care for and commune with this land, and it is my great honor and privilege to care for it. Daily you will find me outside in our garden, taking walks down our driveway, soaking in a yoga practice on our deck, or laying in my hammock. Being sick with Lyme disease made my soul see and hear loud and clear that nature, and taking care of our earth, is one of the very most important ways to connect with oneself. The days I dig my hands into the dirt in my garden, pulling weeds, finding frogs, worms, and other critters, are among my happiest days. They remind me how grateful I am to be alive and to be able to move my body, to touch and feel, and to bring myself to the present moment. What a gift!

Something incredible that also happened during my recovery was rediscovering my love for running. As a child, I loved to run. And I was fast. I pride myself on being the fastest girl runner in the sixth grade (yes, I will still take this as a claim to fame!). But after my dad died, I lost interest in running as I had lost connection with myself. It wasn't until two years after my Lyme disease recovery, when my illness had seemingly gone into "remission," that I thought about taking my daily walks up a notch to a run. I was terrified I would overexert myself and have a Lyme "flare." So, I started slowly. First, it was a jog up and down my driveway just once. Half a mile. I did this for weeks. Later, I moved to one mile and continued for several more weeks. Now, here I am four years later, running an average of fifteen to twenty miles a week! Running outside is a spiritual practice for me, and oftentimes I will open my arms wide mid-run, close my eyes, and feel the breeze and sunshine on my face. Sometimes this act brings me to tears. It is in these moments that I also feel most closely connected to my father's spirit, like he is right there with me, running alongside me.

Never underestimate the power of connection with yourself through nature. A walk. A bike ride. A hike. Just sitting in the sun on your front porch. Even better, take a friend or family member with you to enjoy the experience and connect together!

HEALING PRACTICE

Try starting the conversation with a friend by asking, "How is your heart doing today?" That question is a fast track to sharing feelings between the two of you. Better yet, make time to be with this person outdoors! Journal what the experience was like having an open and authentic conversation with your friend.

"WHEN YOUR HEART AND MIND
ARE BALANCED, AND YOUR BODY
IS IN COMPLETE HARMONY, SO
IS YOUR LIFE."

–KUMAR AAKASH

CHAPTER 10

BALANCED BODY, BALANCED HEART

How often do you feel stress working its way through you? Do you find yourself frequently worried—even as you read this—about making a deadline at work, getting a doctor appointment for your sick child, or taking care of an elderly relative? The list goes on and on. And it's not your imagination—the American Medical Association has said that stress is the number one cause of more than 60 percent of all human illness and disease.

I believe that the stress I was feeling as a perfectionist, a people pleaser, a highly sensitive person, and an overachiever is what resulted in debilitating physical symptoms, and only made my Lyme disease and postpartum depression worse.

I think I was born with a high-stress nature, and it was only amplified the night my dad died when I was eleven. After this traumatic event, I was constantly on high alert for the next catastrophe, and in many ways, I am still undoing and moving through it. Stress was a constant element in my life as a journalist. Covering stories like the latest mass shooting, missing person, and terrorist attack meant that my mind and body were assaulted almost daily with cortisol rushes of stress. When I started balancing life as a business owner with being a mother, it was a match made in heaven for a cortisol overload.

Stress takes a toll on the body, and especially the immune system, as my friend Dr. Marianne Teitelbaum explains. She is a practitioner of Ayurveda, a five-thousand-year-old tradition of holistic medicine that diagnoses with the purpose of understanding the deepest level of imbalance in the body. "When you're under stress, you release a lot of the hormone cortisol, and that shuts down your immune system. That's why you might notice when you get bad news, for example, that stress makes you sick with some kind of infection."

Dr. Teitelbaum uses the ancient herb ashwagandha to balance the neurotransmitters in the brain to stay calm and stop the release of cortisol. I am a huge fan of not only ashwagandha, but many other herbs that Dr. Teitelbaum recommends to help boost our immune system.

When I was sick with Lyme, my physical woes were endless. They included brain fog, chronic fatigue, body shaking, flashing lights in my vision, loss of vision, dizziness, fainting spells, heart palpitations, breathing problems, stomach and digestive distress, extreme weight loss, chronic headaches, nerve pain throughout my body, and so much more. Talk about a mess! I knew that no one medicine was going to fix my deep-rooted issues.

That's where my very dear friend Amber Bodily came in to help. She is a sought-after medical intuitive who is a certified master herbalist and foot zoning practitioner. Amber is able to pinpoint root causes and heal the body on a cellular level from chronic disease and illness. She believes that our bodies have these amazing, magical immune systems that we don't care for or cultivate. "This is why we become very susceptible to sickness and low energy," she says. "When you give the body what it needs, beautiful healing happens in the body. You can get your body back on track."

Amber and I first met over phone consultations, and she tuned into my body to find where I was depleted. Managing stress was one of the main ingredients on my prescription list from Amber. She recommended more yoga and meditation and a calm lifestyle, in addition to the herbs, supplements, and oils.

So, how do you know what your body needs? "Your body is often screaming very loud at you, but you've been taught to ignore it. To tough it out and stay strong. What you really need to do is sit with yourself for a day or two and listen to what it is telling you," says Amber. "Also, think about those stressors in your life and how those are affecting your energy."

Up until that point with Amber, I realized that I had spent most of my life ignoring body signals. I can recall countless times when I would get stressed or anxious and feel a wash of physical symptoms come over me—tingling up the spine, heart palpitations, shortness of breath, even dizziness and faintness. As Amber said, I was taught by society and our culture to ignore these symptoms—just buck up, girlie, and get on with it. I didn't have time to address these physical warning signs that my body was trying to alert me to. And, if anything, now, when I feel the slightest bit off, I go within and **pay attention to what my body is telling me** and often ask it what it needs. What comes up often for me is that I need more sleep, less sugar, and less flour. Amber has taught me to listen to my body, and my hope for you is that you begin to listen to yours, too. Don't feel guilty for taking a nap. If you're tired, take a nap. If you have a headache, lie down and perhaps smell some essential oils.

Ocean Robbins, founder of the Food Revolution Network, is a very busy best-selling author of *The 31-Day Food Revolution*, a conference speaker, and a world-renowned seminar leader. Finding a place of balance for him starts in the morning. "When I'm waking up, I just be, and find a place of stillness, calm, and presence in my heart. I don't start checking my phone first thing." He is kind to his digestive tract, too, by letting it "rest" for a full twelve hours between dinner and breakfast.

FEELING AFFIRMATION

I am feeling what my body is telling me and will listen to what it needs.

"I drink lots of water, green tea, and enjoy foods and herbs that are good for the body."

Ocean also believes that gratitude is one of the most powerful forces in the universe, especially when it comes to taking care of your body. "Take time to pause and be grateful for everything, including the food that is in front of you." He explains that neuroscience has proven that when you cultivate an attitude of gratitude, you actually change the chemistry of your brain in ways that create peace, ease, joy, flow, and satisfaction in life, which helps your nervous system to be calm and reduces stress.

"There are studies showing that people who took five minutes a day to write down three things they were grateful for enjoyed great benefits, such as longer marriages, longer lives, they exercised more, they lost weight. They felt better about themselves, and they did better things with their lives," says Ocean. "One thing that the pandemic showed is how grateful we are for human connections, especially the physical ones such as hugs and handshakes."

I started my gratitude practice in the throes of Lyme disease, when all I could do was lie in bed and sulk. But I really wanted something to be hopeful for. So I grabbed a journal and pen, and started writing down things I was grateful for, even though I felt robbed of life. My kids were healthy. It was a beautiful day outside. I have a great marriage. I work for myself and therefore didn't need to take a sick leave of absence from work. Staring back at my gratitude journal, even when I felt like I was knocking on death's door, caused me to pause and rethink my mindset about my life that day. It made me feel something I had been lacking— just a tiny bit of hope. I kept up the journaling almost daily during my darkest days, and began to notice the shift in my mind and body.

A regular gratitude practice quickly gets you out of any "victim" mindset and cycle of pity—at least it did for me. As I write this, I'm on spring break in a gorgeous mountain house with my family. I woke up feeling groggy, a bit off, and grumpy. After a forty-five-minute yoga practice, I turned to my gratitude journal and wrote down everything I was grateful for. Gorgeous mountains and mountain air. A healthy family in the middle of a pandemic. A team that I trust to handle my company while I take a week off from work. I took a look back and breathed a deep sigh and felt an immediate, positive shift in mood.

For me, journaling, yoga, and creating a gratitude list helps keep my anxiety and stress from overwhelming my system. But each person needs to find their own tool kit of stress-reducing activities. One of the most inspirational people I spoke to for this book is Dr. Courtney Howard, an emergency physician in Yellowknife, in Canada's subarctic, and a clinical associate professor in the Cumming School of Medicine at the University of Calgary. She is a nationally and globally recognized expert on the impacts of climate change on health. Her husband, Dr. Darcy Scott, is a pediatrician in that remote city of twenty thousand that is the medical hub for the province, and was the medical director for the region throughout COVID-19. "We have all these teensy, tiny, little indigenous communities that are thousands of kilometers from our care. We had to think about how to prevent the virus from getting into these little communities, as we had a limited number of medevac planes to get patients to a ventilator if necessary," Dr. Howard explains. Clearly, this is not my or your daily stress about driving a carpool!

To keep stress at bay, Dr. Howard says that exercise is the big one for her. "I really need that dopamine boost every day. And so I do exercise pretty much every single day, not necessarily for a long time. That really keeps me on an even keel. I know that once I've done that, I can take care of other people. Sleep is important, as well as getting outside into nature."

I can't speak enough to the health and well-being benefits of a regular daily exercise routine. Exercise releases endorphins, those hormones that act as natural relaxers in the body and actually improve your sleep.

Before Lyme disease brought me to my knees, I was a Zumba instructor and absolutely loved the energy and freedom of creative movement with exciting beats. I loved the flair of a salsa dance, the flow of a cumbia, and the beats of the music. I had also spent most of my teens and twenties teaching ballet, tap, and hip-hop to young children, something I loved! Today, because I love variety, I tend to hop between yoga, weights, dance, barre, CrossFit, and running. My mind constantly needs something new. But I make a point to move my body almost daily.

In addition to exercise, I've learned that sleep is one of the most important things you can do for your body to allow it to heal. Unfortunately, our society tells us to go-go-go, that sleep isn't a big priority, and I fell victim to this mentality, hard. As a network TV producer, I was used to four hours of sleep a night and would often fight the urge to sleep, which trained me for the sleepless nights in the newborn years. Though I constantly felt tired, I ignored my body and the signals it was giving me. Sleep was for "wussies." I didn't need it, I told myself. My second daughter, Kate, didn't sleep through the night for a full year. I know that took an enormous toll on my body and mental well-being. These days, I make sure I get at least eight to nine hours of sleep a night, while leaving my phone in another room. On the weekends, if I feel a nap is needed (and usually it is!), I take one.

When I'm feeling stressed, my yoga mat is my go-to place, where I let myself feel all my feelings and breathe through them. Maybe because I'm doing physical movement at the same time, my yoga practice helps me move and breathe through my feelings as well. "There's something about quieting the noise around you and looking inward that helps you connect with your higher self," says my friend Carolan Hoffman, owner of Hot Spot Dupont, a yoga studio in Washington, D.C.

You may choose a yoga mat or some other safe space to do your inner work, but the principle of it remains the same—moving and breathing through your emotions:

- On your mat, as you begin your practice (either sitting down or standing), close your eyes and invite your messy emotions and suffering into your heart. Whatever emotions you've been ignoring, acknowledge them. Even speak to them in a compassionate tone: "I see you, and we are going to work through this together."

- Once you've acknowledged any upsetting emotions, observe how it feels in your body. Do you feel pain any where? Is your chest tight? How is your breathing?

- Imagine you are looking at yourself from the other side of the room and observe your physical self.

- Let these emotions and any pain move through your body through the power of breath and movement. Picture them crashing against a rocky shore as a form of release. Don't be tempted to stop them; just ride them no matter how uneasy it may feel. My yoga practice often leaves me sobbing in a primal and healing way.

- Visualize yourself leaving those emotions behind and moving toward a more peaceful state of being. And don't skip that Shavasana, the final resting pose in a yoga practice!

If I can get on my mat, I have won the day. The gentle movement through breathing and focus on feelings for even ten minutes is enough to help me move through the stress of the kids being on my nerves, sad memories about my dad, worries about my Lyme recurrence, and the pressing work deadlines. I feel balanced in my body and balanced in my heart, and so can you. Namaste.

HEALING PRACTICE

Keep a gratitude journal nearby (such as at your bedside) and practice the act of gratitude daily. At the end of each day, or even in the beginning of the day, write down everything you are grateful for—the good things that have happened to you and what good things lie ahead. Finish each gratitude entry with the line "I see good things and many possibilities ahead."

DAILY PERMISSION
TO FEEL

"THE PRIVILEGE OF A
LIFETIME IS TO BECOME
WHO YOU REALLY ARE."

–CARL JUNG

CHAPTER 11

DISCOVER YOUR DEEPER, POWERFUL SELF

We've all been through storms. We will all face more of them in the future. That's just part of being alive on this planet. As you know by now, my big storms were my father's abrupt death and my diagnosis and struggle with Lyme disease. I'm hoping yours were not as devastating. As difficult as our challenges can be, it's moving through the eye of the storm that makes us wiser and more resilient.

The pandemic is one storm we all have in common, and the collective trauma of the loss of "normal," grieving for people we've lost, anxiety for our own personal safety, and economic pain is something that will take healing for years to come. I interviewed many of the health and wellness experts in this book during the 2020 lockdown. Most of them agreed that one of the silver linings of the pandemic was that people were forced to sit with themselves and consider their lives and what gave them meaning.

"I think this became a time to uncover what you really want in your life, and what you want to contribute," says my friend and favorite yogi Carolan Hoffman. "When we're busy in life, like we were before the

FEELING AFFIRMATION

*I am my own source of joy
and love in this world.*

pandemic, most people don't have time to think. They were running on everybody else's demands."

Lyme disease, like the pandemic, caused me to literally stop and rethink much of how I had lived—the avoidance of feeling my feelings, my people-pleasing tendencies, and my lack of self-care. I sometimes refer to this as the "gift of Lyme." I hear other people refer to their health struggles as the "gift of cancer." While I don't wish for a health issue or another pandemic on any of us, I do believe all of us need to intentionally step back from our lives and other people from time to time, and look inside for guidance from our heart. We're the only ones who can journey within ourselves; we have to "walk the walk" alone to our true selves. It can feel lonely, I know.

"That loneliness you feel is trying to instruct you to go somewhere a little deeper," says Carolan. "You start out on the surface, and if you dive a little bit deeper into that pond, you move closer toward your heart and what it is telling you. You realize that you are the source of joy and love in your life. Suddenly every relationship becomes better when you have a more connected one with yourself."

When I started connecting more to my heart, to listening to it, I began to feel my self-worth improve. I think this is what I was lacking in myself throughout my life. In a way, I became a friend to myself. I became a mother to myself. I learned to speak to myself with the same compassion I give to others. We need to be a friend to ourselves first before we can be a good friend to others. And that starts by getting honest with yourself.

My relationships with people and friends are deeper than ever before because of this deeper work. I'm learning to love myself, love me for ME, and in turn, serve the world with that love. It's a beautiful process. By getting honest with myself, I've also been able to get honest and vulnerable with my friends. We live in a society and culture where we're not honest about how we are really feeling. The question "How are you?" is really an empty, meaningless question in our culture. So, I've started to get honest with it when people ask me. Sometimes I don't wait for people to ask. The other day, I found myself feeling low and depressed, and I couldn't pinpoint why. I meditated, did yoga, and felt the urge to reach out to a friend and tell her how I was feeling, so I did. That text to her led to us getting together for a long walk a few days later to talk and catch up. Being honest, open, and vulnerable with her fed my soul and led to an even deeper, meaningful connection.

My former client and friend Ocean Robbins suggests that there are two times during the day when you can take even just a few minutes to connect to your inner self: right upon waking and right before sleep. Start by making these sacred, special times in your day. Ocean Robbins uses every morning to take a "moral inventory" of his life. "I find a place of stillness, calm, and presence in my heart, rather than checking my phone." He also turns off all devices by 7:00 p.m., and doesn't engage in work activities after 9:00 p.m.

Entering your sleep with the right mindset is suggested by Rajshree Patel, an international self-awareness coach, teacher, speaker, and author of *The Power of Vital Force*. Rajshree, otherwise known as "Raj," has guided government leaders, Fortune 500 executives, and individuals from all walks of life on how tapping into their personal power can achieve true results.

Raj suggests that, as you enter your sleep, when you've turned off the lights, you take this time to really let go and not hold on to the negative feelings of the day. "The more we hold on to what has happened, the deeper the impact of the situation on us," she explains. How many times have you laid in bed replaying everything in your mind with a dialogue such as, "I should have done this," or "Why didn't I think of that?" We beat ourselves up for our past behaviors or feelings, creating an invitation for more of the same in the future. You did the best you could; now let it go.

Right as you fall asleep, use a little breath work to let things go. Take five to ten long conscious breaths, in and out. This helps you enter sleep by releasing the negative self-talk and closing the files in your brain that are draining your power. Entering sleep with negative feelings will not serve you tomorrow. A new day is a new possibility. Don't waste it with a "hangover" of negative feelings about yourself.

I know that, for me, being alone for the first time without noise and with just my inner self was scary. It is still often scary for me! But once I experienced how this quiet alone time started to change my relationship with myself and how I show up in the world, I started actually craving it more.

Here are some tips I use to quiet the noise around me and dive into my deeper, truer self.

- TURN OFF SOCIAL MEDIA. In January 2019, I took a social media hiatus for one month. I loved it so much, I took another social media hiatus in January 2020. What I noticed was that my opinions became my own again. I wasn't influenced by others, nor did I feel overloaded with news, information, and the comparison to how others were living their lives. It is one of the healthiest things I've done for my mental health, and I encourage you to try it, even if it is for one week.

- STOP CHECKING THE NEWS. I'm a former network TV producer, so checking the news is second nature to me. When I was suffering from Lyme, at first all I could do was read news stories and blogs about other people who had suffered from Lyme. This was never helpful, so I just stopped. In the same way, I encourage you to stop reading stories about those suffering from coronavirus, or even stories about symptoms. Yes, it is good to be informed; therefore, turn to the CDC, or perhaps some news site, and let that be it.

○ **DIGITALLY DISCONNECT.** At least for a few hours every day. My husband and I started a tradition in that we now disconnect from our phones every night from 5:00 p.m. until 7:00 p.m., and sometimes longer. We want to be present for our family and our children, and this goes a long way in maintaining our health, and also being an example to our children to be present.

Choosing how we show up in the world is also a big part of Raj's work. "So many of us have avoided the internal noise or dialogue, whether it's self-deprecation or harsh judgments about ourselves," she says. "It's almost like the pandemic created this greater universal consciousness and asked each of us to look within."

When we quiet the noise around us, our personal power ignites. We each have our own power inside of us—it's accessed by going within to unleash our own insights, creativity, and imagination. It's trusting our feelings to guide us to a life of meaning and purpose, and make choices that are right for ourselves and others and us. For me, accessing my personal power means that I'm never alone even if I am physically alone.

Sometimes when we look within, we find things we don't like about ourselves, whether it's how we've behaved toward family, colleagues, or even toward ourselves. "The first step when looking within is acceptance of yourself," says Raj. "From that place of acceptance, you can start to have honest conversations with oneself. It's very important that one start to look inward, and to recognize that you're not just your achievements. It's important to recognize you, your spirit, consciousness, has to be greater than your achievements. If it was the other way around, you couldn't achieve it. That is who and how powerful you truly are."

Raj suggests that when your identity is connected to something greater than accomplishments or achievements, then you're able to truly heal. Staying connected to your identity that comes from within is what helps you move through a trauma or storm in a more resilient way.

When I was going through Lyme disease, I was determined not to have my identity be defined by it. I knew I was more than this illness. Yet I also realize how hard it is to get to that place of knowing you are more than your trauma, your loss, or your illness. When I was stripped of my health, and therefore the ability to be a present parent and wife, I was stripped of everything. The identity question was blaring, "Who am I if I am not well? If I am not able to parent? WHO really is Ashley?"

Dr. Bhargave, author of the book *A Moment of Insight* (whom we met in chapter 4) believes that we all can answer the question of "Who am I?" by identifying our five primary gifts—these are the qualities that really form the inner core, or DNA, of our very being. Once you identify your five gifts, they keep you focused and centered on who you are innately, not letting yourself be defined by others. It shifts the narrative from the "not good enough" we hear from others and even ourselves to "I am worthy as I am." Once you know and use your gifts in the world, it also helps you to live your life in a more purposeful way. Here are some ways you can begin to identify your unique gifts:

- What did you love to do most as a child?
- What are you most excited to do as an adult?
- What values are you most passionate about (health, relationships, etc.)?
- What do friends, family, and coworkers say is most unique about you?

It took me a long time to honor myself as a unique human being with special gifts that provide myself and others with resilience. I'm hoping you're inspired by some of this chapter's insights to go deep inside and uncover your own.

HEALING PRACTICE

Make a list of your five unique gifts, using the space below. Some things may fall off and others may be added to your list. Then place the list in a spot that you can easily see every day. Having this list will give you a balanced awareness of who you are, and also guide you in using these gifts and live a more powerful and purposeful life.

"HAPPY PEOPLE BUILD THEIR
INNER WORLD; UNHAPPY PEOPLE
BLAME THEIR OUTER WORLD."

–BUDDHA

CHAPTER 12

STRENGTH OF A SPIRITUAL PRACTICE

One of the most popular TED Talks about overcoming trauma is by writer and mental health activist Andrew Solomon, which is titled "How the Worst Moments in Our Lives Make Us Who We Are." He tells his story of the pain and unhappiness he suffered as a young boy who struggled with his sexual identity throughout his entire childhood. Yet he says he wouldn't trade being teased and even harassed by his peers because "these terrible events have made me the person I am today." Andrew goes on to say with tremendous grace and even humor, "You need to take the traumas and make them part of who you've come to be, and you need to fold the worst events of your life into a narrative of triumph, evincing a better self in response to things that hurt."

Although I've wished a million times over that my father hadn't died when I was so young, overcoming my emotional challenges has changed my narrative in a positive way in so many parts of my life. I've become a more compassionate friend, emotionally engaged mother, and patient spouse. I've also become a more spiritual person, which has made me all of these things and more. It's been a long and circuitous route as I've wound my way through formal religion, to no religion, to finally arriving at a place where my spirituality practice is what I lean on to "evince a better self," as Andrew Solomon says.

I was raised from a young age to be a Catholic, but I didn't fully connect with the religion. Both of my parents were Catholic, and my grandparents, who I loved dearly, were devout Catholics. They went to mass in Latin, and my grandpa made rosaries to send to children around the world. I went to Catholic school on and off in my early life, and like many other young girls at that time, hated the restrictions on my creativity with the uniforms! I couldn't wear jewelry and express myself in the way I wanted to. I didn't (and still don't) believe that children need to be forced at age seven to repent of their sins in an enclosed booth to a priest. I'll never forget my first penance at that age trying to come up with my "sins" to tell the priest: "I pulled my sister's hair. I stole my sister's toy." I was ordered to pray eight Hail Marys, ten Our Fathers, and be on my way. Oh, if a priest could hear my sins now!

In middle school, after my dad died, I was done being Catholic. I felt totally betrayed by God. What kind of God would rob me of my dad? It was then that my friend Jenn invited me to her Nazarene Church, a Christian denomination where I learned a much more open and expressive way to love God. I sang in the teen youth group, starred in the church musicals, and went to camp. I loved the friends I made, and loved the new relationship I had started to form with God.

But like many young adults, when I went off to college, I retreated from any formal religion and stayed away from God, or any kind of higher power, for a long time. I didn't need religion, or spirituality, I thought. By the time I arrived in New York City as an aspiring journalist, I had completely lost any kind of spiritual anchor. I thought I was sailing along in life under my own power. Boy, was I wrong.

It wasn't until my Lyme disease that I learned I need to lean on something that was bigger and wiser than I was. Call it a God, a divine being, a higher power, a source of light—I felt a strong calling to find a spiritual practice that would uplift and sustain me in terrible times. I wanted to get back to God, or some version of a higher power. On one hand, I liked the sacred aspects of the formal Catholic Church. But I sought something with less doctrine and fewer restrictive customs, more personal and open to all people.

So, I joined a Methodist church near our home, and I found a spiritual community of support during my Lyme struggles. I got back to singing again with the choir. People brought my family dinners during weeks when I felt especially low on energy. It was a safe space for me to start to ask questions about God, and even question the role of a formal religion in my life.

Being the intensely curious person I am, I continued to explore what the right "formula" was for spirituality in my life. It was then that I met LeeAnn Taylor, a spiritual mentor and author of one of my favorite books, *The Fragile Face of God: A True Story About Light, Darkness, and the Hope Beyond the Veil*. She is the mother of five children, three of whom were born with autism and fragile X syndrome, a genetic disorder that causes severe mental impairment.

LeeAnn taught me a whole different way to incorporate spirituality into my life. "People mix up religion and spirituality," LeeAnn explains, "but spirituality is a personal practice instead of a set of doctrines that are typically part of a formal religion." The personal connection piece is what I felt had been missing.

The beauty of a spiritual practice, LeeAnn explains, is that it is different for everyone and absolutely personal in choice. "People that I work with often come from some type of religious background, but they eventually found themselves seeking something deeper, more personal, and immediate." Being spiritual means you recognize there is something greater than yourself, and you commit to tapping into that "Spirit" or "God" or "Divine Power" to create more significance and meaning in

FEELING AFFIRMATION

God (Source/Spirit/Divine) is always available to me. I am never alone and feel peace and comfort in knowing there is an unseen world ready to support and love me beyond this human life.

your life. Writing this book, for instance, was me answering a spiritual calling to share my hard-earned wisdom with others.

LeeAnn has taught me so much about accessing spirit (my choice of words to explain a greater source of wisdom). A lot of my work with LeeAnn has been practicing the art of sacred writing. And let me tell you, I feel more connected spiritually using this writing process than sitting in a confessional booth. In many ways, the practice of sacred writing is similar to the practice of discernment in Christianity, where you ask God for guidance in decision-making.

Sacred writing starts with the simplest of tools, a notebook and a pen. And then you pose to yourself a heart-centered question on the page. It can be a simple question such as, "Spirit, what will you have me know?" As you write, you keep pausing and listening, pausing and listening, and then writing whatever you feel is coming, whatever you feel prompted to say, whatever nuance of an idea is there. And even if it just feels like a journal entry and a free-write session, just write it, just write it. And before long, you'll start to discern that there's a voice there.

"The voice on the page, in some ways, is not your own," explains LeeAnn. "It is a wisdom that is independent of you. Sacred writing is the foundation of revelation. It is a tangible way to access your spirit through a question that you pose to yourself. But as you get more confident in leaning in and trusting your spirit, you will begin to listen for and hear the question that you need to ask."

LeeAnn taught me that when I listen for the question, I can write that question with greater wisdom, which will in turn reveal what the spirit has in store for me. One thing I did during the pandemic was to get very honest with myself about my drinking habit. I had developed a nightly "glass of wine or two" habit that, in my soul, I knew needed to stop. I would write about it in my sacred journal and ask my spirit about it. The answer I always got back was, You must stop drinking. Drinking no longer serves you. The answer got louder and louder each time I wrote it.

So, I stopped. Has it been easy? No. But by getting honest with myself, I have allowed myself to become a friend to myself first, and therefore a better friend to others.

"Listening for the question and giving it an honest answer is that next layer of internal wisdom and leaping into a greater relationship with the divine," LeeAnn says. "It's just so simple to access. It is not difficult."

For me, sacred writing is so beautiful because I don't need to be in a cathedral to practice it. I don't need any kind of special education. I can do it in my living room, my kitchen, my garden. "The divine is constantly available and awaiting your inquiry, and absolutely delights with the opportunity and the privilege to have an audience with you, to communicate with you, and to bring you the wisdom and the answers and the knowledge that you seek," says LeeAnn.

I know what some of you may be thinking now: "How in the heck will I know my spirit when I see it? Or feel it?" Most people think of the spirit as God, a divine being like a heavenly mother or father, or something that is a higher-power figure. "Think of the spirit or divine as your ancestors, or your loved ones who have passed over, and are still guiding you. Their role is to lead you and help you," says LeeAnn. She gives the example of her mother who died when she was eight. "I have this relationship with my mother that is stronger and more integrative now than it ever was when she was here," says LeeAnn. "And so sometimes I'll say [the] spirit taught me this, and I'm referring to Mother. Sometimes I'm referring to the divine. Sometimes I'm referring to other relatives who have passed over. Sometimes this refers to your guides who may not have been ancestors, but friends or, um, celestial experts, as it were—angels. So it really is kind of this beautiful, simple, general term that could mean any number of those individuals."

I have several guides I regularly talk to. My guardian angel is one. I have seen her and spoken to her in meditations. My soul is another, and I know she speaks to me through sacred writing. I speak to my dad and maternal grandma and grandpa through sacred writing. I talk to them in my head throughout the day, and I always know that when I see a blue jay or hear a certain song on the radio like Charlie Puth's "See You Again" that my grandma is saying hello!

As LeeAnn taught me, spirits are not vulnerable to the states of confusion, fear, and despair that we have here on Earth as human beings. "Spirits have continuous access to clarity, peace, and understanding," says LeeAnn. "You have an immediate and personal front-row seat to access that wisdom. And that is the source of unbelievable strength and power."

My spiritual practice has taught me so much, especially how to find lasting hope and joy in the darkest hours. It has helped me trust that I can seek guidance on almost any issue that is gnawing at me. My practice evolves daily, but if I go several days or a week without it, I feel lonely and alone in the world.

"The beauty of a spiritual practice is that it helps us realize that we are more than all of this. We are greater than the script or narrative that we are going through at the time," says LeeAnn.

Boy, does that give me power, strength, and joy.

HEALING PRACTICE

Start each day with a "heart check"—the most important conversation you have each day is with yourself. Make a conscious choice to live the day ahead with compassion for all and hope for your life. Journal how your heart is feeling today.

"IN MY VIEW, THE BEST OF HUMANITY IS IN OUR EXERCISE OF EMPATHY AND COMPASSION."

–SARAH McBRIDE

CHAPTER 13

EXERCISE YOUR EMPATHY

Ever had those days when you keep replaying your fears, anxieties, and problems over and over in your head? Your mind is stuck on a spin cycle and you can't let go of negative and worrying thoughts? It's very easy to fall into a "woe is me" mindset. As you've heard me say, I'm an empath, and super sensitive to other people's energies and comments. I can get thrown into a blue mood very easily based on the energy of other people, how they react to me, and what they say to me. It is hard for me not to take things personally, even in business and running a company.

What I bring myself back to when this happens is to focus on the power of kindness toward others. Because guess what? That is the surest path to getting out of your own head and improving your own well-being by exercising your empathy muscle.

One of the most amazing books I've read in the last few years is Jamil Zaki's *The War for Kindness*. Jamil is a professor of psychology at Stanford University and the director of the Stanford Social Neuroscience Laboratory. His book features cutting-edge research that shows that empathy is something we can call upon to strengthen ourselves, our relationships, and our health itself.

"In most cases, empathy benefits everyone involved," Jamil says. "For instance, patients of empathic doctors are more satisfied with their relationship, and are also more likely to follow doctors' recommendations, which is important for things like preventative care. And spouses of empathic partners are happier in their marriages." He notes that the one big thing people don't realize is that those who show empathy for others also benefit themselves. "It's not just receiving kindness, but giving it helps us, too. So, people who are relatively high in empathy, for instance, are less likely to become depressed. Feeling empathy for others reduces our stress, too."

Empathy is a powerful medicine in my life. I make it a daily habit to be intentional about how I want to show up in the world every day. Each morning, I use Brendon Burchard's *High Performance Planner*, which asks you to choose one word to express the kind of person you want to be that day. My choice is almost always "kind." I want to look for ways to show kindness, compassion, and empathy to myself and others.

The challenge is to call upon our virtuous selves to show empathy for others instead of falling into victim mode. Jamil calls it the battle of the vicious cycle vs. the virtuous cycle. "The vicious cycle is that when we feel totally stressed and depleted, we often feel like we don't even have the bandwidth for ourselves right now, let alone for other people. And so we decide to focus on ourselves," he explains.

The problem with that, he notes, is that, oftentimes, we are missing out on the benefit of giving to others, which in turn comes back to us. When we decide that we don't have room for other people, we actually are depriving ourselves of one of the best avenues to feeling better and doing better.

"The virtuous cycle is when we can break out of that mistake, and understand that the times you feel that you least have energy for others is the time that you should work hardest to find that energy for them," Jamil says. "When we can make that choice, we can actually feel ourselves pulling out of the intense self-focus that can derail our happiness."

I know I often end up happier when I help others. It's amazing how I can move from feeling stressed and not having room for one more thing, and then I show a simple act of kindness toward someone else, and I feel stronger and more centered in my own life.

"In the age that we're living in right now, it is sometimes harder to find and make those kindness connections," explains Jamil. "We all have kindness challenges, and I think that's because we put pressure on ourselves to help someone in a big, dramatic way like giving a significant amount of money or knitting them a sweater. People think of giving like it's a performance, something that has to be done exactly right. But the people receiving could care less about the details. So I think that one of the big principles here is to lower the bar for ourselves."

As a people-pleasing perfectionist, that's advice that goes straight to my heart. One way I show kindness to myself in a small way is to give myself a day of rest once in a while if I'm feeling low energy. Not every day has to be a contest of how much I've achieved or crossed off my to-do list. With my girlfriends, I am intentional about both texting them to check in, but also to make plans to go for a walk and connect in person. And one of the most rewarding things I've done recently is to deliver lasagna dinners to families in need through a local program called Lasagna Love. And my favorite thing to do as a mother is write thank-you notes to my daughters, telling them how much I love them.

"Sometimes being kind is just doing 1 percent more than you are already doing, like baking an extra dozen cookies for someone or ordering an extra take-out meal for a neighbor," Jamil reminds us. "Just take what you are already doing and pivot it a bit more toward someone else, and the effect is really wonderful." These small acts of kindness are the quickest and surest ways to get me out of the chatter in my head that is so depleting emotionally and physically. Exercising your empathy in these ways feeds your soul.

And you know what the most empathetic thing of all is? Just listening to someone. Holding space for them and their feelings. It can feel like that's not enough, but it is often exactly what our friends and family want most from us. I am mindful about pausing my work and other responsibilities to sit with my daughters and let them know I am here for them, and checking in on how they are feeling about all the little (and big) events in their lives. Sometimes all they say is, "All good, Mom!" But other times, this checking in leads to very emotionally connecting conversations that bring us closer.

Parents can improve their children's empathy muscle for others as well. And one of the best ways to do this is by exposing them to storytelling through the arts. Research shows that stories have tremendous power in changing neural pathways and opening up our minds and hearts to others.

I'm a big believer in the arts as a way to connect to the feelings of others, and in doing so, helping to improve our own moods. Jamil discusses the arts as a community and relationship builder in his book. My friend Dan DeLuca is an award-winning TV actor who starred in the popular musical *Newsies*. When not performing, he shares with others his belief in the healing and connecting power of the arts.

Dan says that as early as 500 BC, ancient Egyptians encouraged people suffering with mental blocks to engage in artistic interests and attend concerts and dances. "The aim was to potentially break through some negative feelings, and channel energy to create a life of wholeness." He notes that ancient Greeks also used drama and music to promote healthy mood shifts. In the late 1800s, psychiatrist Sigmund Freud pioneered the use of humor and artistic practices into his work with patients. And in more modern times, the founder of psychodrama, Jacob Moreno, developed a role reversal method in the early 1920s where a person would assume the form of another to develop compassion for that person.

FEELING AFFIRMATION

I am an empathetic person, and I believe in using that power to heal both myself and others.

"Storytelling and the arts help us play out the arc of our lives," says Dan. "We listen to the music of our childhood to feel the safety of simpler times. We'll watch romantic comedy movies to fashion our own journey from dating to marriage. Using the arts as a healing process has always been a driving force in my life."

Arts are a big part of our family life, as they were in my childhood. My mother was a professional ballet dancer, and still owns a dance studio at the age of seventy-two. Dance has always been a way of expressing my feelings and communicating without words to other people. My daughters and I frequently make up dances together to fit the mood of the day. Dance movement to me has always been a powerful form of story and connection to a higher power.

Dan reminds us that engaging in the arts isn't as difficult as you think, even if you don't consider yourself artistic. It can be as simple as decorating your home or choosing just the right clothes to wear to a celebration party. Here are some ways Dan "rewires" his mind to be more positive and empathetic to himself and others.

- **WRITE A NEW STORY ABOUT YOUR LIFE.** Being a performer, Dan likes to think of his life as a movie. He suggests journaling yourself as a new character. Be specific about the strengths of the new you, and how you will make healthier and happier choices in your daily life, including exercising that empathy muscle with others.

- **MAKE A PLAYLIST OF UPBEAT MUSIC.** Dan considers music an "invisible magic force," and a quick and tangible way to alter your mood in almost any moment. Best of all, listen and dance to music with others as a way to connect.

- **ACT LIKE A CHILD AGAIN.** Adults lose the joy and wonder of being a child as they age. So play in the sand, color with crayons, make silly decorations just for fun. Dan notes that a Harvard study asked eight elderly men to spend five days at a retreat to act twenty years younger. Among the results, the men had improved in mental function and body flexibility.

HEALING PRACTICE

Practice empathy by doing one small act of kindness a day for someone else for a week. Note in your journal how you felt before you showed empathy, and afterward.

"HOPE IS A VERB."

—DAVID ORR,
ENVIRONMENTALIST AND ACTIVIST

CHAPTER 14

IMAGINING YOUR HOPEFUL SELF

I wrote this book during the deepest, darkest days of the pandemic. As I mentioned in the chapter on spirituality, having come from a place of deep healing, I felt called to share my journey with others and to offer you, my reader, the ability to access your own authentic power and find hope in healing for any type of life adversity you may face.

I recognized the emotions I experienced during the pandemic—the fear, anxiety, loss, and grief—as the same ones that I felt during my father's death, Lyme disease, and postpartum depression. Instead of falling into the same emotional hole as I had during those traumas, I now had built up a reservoir of strength and resiliency that I could keep filling with the techniques I had learned from all the guides and healers you've met in the book.

The outside noise of the world and daily "bad news" headlines can make it extremely challenging to keep our eyes focused on the endgame—living our lives by being true to our feelings and inner guides. I believe that when you stay centered on your heart's messages to yourself, your life becomes filled with great possibilities. You can look to the future with hope.

As Ocean Robbins says, "Hope is not just a noun. It's a verb. It's something that comes from actions you take and choices you make, and ways that you live and the future that you invest in." He explains that it is so easy for us to hop on the fear roller coaster every day, where we focus on how many ways things can get worse. "That's a dead end. I want to challenge all of us to step into hope as an action, as a choice, as something we author in our lives."

I love his suggestion of starting each day with the vision of where you want to go. And then coming up with small steps or a map of sorts to move forward. "You've got to keep moving and developing sustainable habits," Ocean says. "It's your habits day in and day out that will create a healthy foundation to get you through the times of being exhausted, worn out, and stressed." Getting into the habit of beginning each day from the heart is such a powerful way to keep hopeful for the day ahead and the future beyond.

Both Ocean and Dr. Gathers, whom you met in Chapter 8, gently remind us that our journey is not about getting to perfect, but focusing on making progress one step at a time. "Healing is a lifelong process," says Dr. Gathers. "I'm not 100 percent completely healed from anything. I've just done a lot of the work. Because of this work, I have a healthier perspective and am way more comfortable living in my power than eight or ten years ago."

When I think about how far I've come in my journey to healing, I'm brought to tears. I look at little eleven-year-old Ashley, who had just lost her father. She was so scared, confused, hurt, and felt so abandoned. Teenage Ashley wanted and sought love from everyone, and in especially unhealthy places, as did young adult Ashley. She was insecure, felt shame, and was uncomfortable in her own skin. In some ways, I still am uncomfortable in my own skin, and it is a daily process I am learning about in a beautiful way.

LeeAnn Taylor, who has faced the utmost challenge of raising three children with a severe genetic disease, says that "even in the midst of that

FEELING AFFIRMATION

*I am much wiser and stronger than the
challenges I will face in life.*

heaviness, my work is to keep myself above it, and live in a lighter, more hopeful space." What I've learned from LeeAnn's story is that no one can choose what challenges life presents us with, but we have 100 percent control over how we handle the things that come our way. "Life is a path of learning," she says. "You may be afraid and confused, but yet you need to know that you are so much more than the challenge you have. Your wiser self will help you see that, and you will make it through."

My challenges change daily, as I'm sure yours do, too. Some days they are silly and almost ridiculous, like arguing with my daughter over wanting to eat too many unhealthy snacks. (Seriously, how many jelly beans can a child eat without turning into one?) Other days, my challenge is keeping myself from the pull of underlying sadness, and even depression, over my father's death and worries about triggering my Lyme disease again. Then there's client deadlines, managing employees, nurturing my marriage . . . It's hard to find a day when things seem to be running smoothly. We all seek a level of stability in our daily lives, but the truth is, we're like little boats being tossed around on the ocean each day. And some waves are just way bigger than others.

These are some of the resiliency tools I use, and my hope is that they will work for you, too:

- Keep in conversation with yourself.
- Listen to your heart—it's wiser than your brain.
- Give yourself permission to feel all your feelings.
- Call upon your spiritual guides and a Higher Power.
- Live with empathy and compassion for yourself and others.
- Get out in nature. Get your toes in the grass, go on a walk, and commune with the natural world around you. Love the earth back and take care of it.

My hope is that you are walking away with an empowering thought process and guide for dealing with the messy aspects of life, and a new way to uncover a beautiful, authentic you. Because as I said in the beginning of this book, a mess will happen—you can count on that. It is how we allow ourselves to process and feel through the mess, the adversities, the heartbreak, and the grief that determines whether true healing happens.

Remember, friend: Don't try to be strong when you're not feeling it.

Remember that it is okay to be *not so strong*. In fact, I want you to embrace it. Give yourself permission to feel all of the feelings that come flooding into your mind and heart.

And those messy feelings you're feeling throughout the day? Or during an uncomfortable or sad situation? Don't bury them. And if you've already buried them, it's not too late. I promise they're still there. Use the F.E.E.L. Framework and other practices in this book to move through them.

Hold your heart, and know that I'm holding your hand with you through this journey.

You've got this. There's always a reason to be hopeful, and accessing your own authentic power is the path to get you there.

HEALING PRACTICE

Start each day with a "heart check"—the most important
conversation you have each day is with yourself.
Make a conscious choice to live the day ahead with
compassion for all, and hope for your life.

ACKNOWLEDGMENTS

It is hard to think of where to start when I consider all the people who have brought me to the path of healing and hope, and who helped contribute to this book.

First, I want to thank God, my "Higher Power," the Divine, for providing me with the courage to put words on paper. This book was divinely inspired and came to life through a deep calling through prayer and meditation. Thank you, God, for the honor and privilege to be a catalyst in the message of hope and healing, and having me serve as a conduit in sharing this message with the world.

Thank you to my dear "ESP" Julie Reisler, who helped me tap into my own inner knowing and uncover what the universe had in store for me: this book! This book wouldn't have been born without your gentle loving guidance and support.

To my dear friend Dr. Emma Seppälä, for advising and guiding me through this process in your loving and gentle way, and for contributing your wisdom in the foreword. I am forever grateful for our friendship and for your unconditional love and support.

To the experts who took the time to speak with me and share their wisdom in this book, many of whom have helped me on my own personal path to authentic power and healing, I am eternally and profoundly grateful.

To the fabulous team at kn literary, who supported and guided me in the art of storytelling, and especially to my dear partner in this project: Melinda Cross—what a joy to be on this journey with you. Thank you.

To my incredible team at Nardi Media, I continue to be in awe of us as we grow and help spread the message of our experts to the world. I am so grateful and honored to be working among the most talented and creative minds in the business. What a joy it is to wake up every day and be excited to go to work and serve our clients! And to my Nardi Media clients, many of whom were interviewed for this book and have become my dear friends. What an honor and privilege we have to elevate your messages to the world. Thank you for trusting our team to spread your voices to the masses using the power of the media.

Sarah Kaler, for coaching and guiding me to be the best leader possible to the Nardi Media team while also honoring my mind, body, and spirit.

Lucinda Halpern and Kelly Notaras, for the unconditional support, love, and guidance in all things business, books, and life.

I am beyond grateful for my girlfriends and the endless laughter, support, and memories, and especially for all of the people (including family, church members, friends, and strangers) who helped support me during my darkest days. Your kindness and compassion will forever be a part of my healing.

To the Collective Book Studio, thank you for helping me birth this book to the world and for your enthusiastic support and guidance behind it.

To my mom, "Nana," and sister, Alexandra, thank you for being my biggest cheerleaders in life, and for being open to the idea of sharing our profound loss so that others may find hope and healing in their own lives. Alexandra, Tommy, and Wells, I am so grateful for you three (almost four!). Thank you for always providing me with constant laughter and love!

Giggie and Papa, Jill, Chris, Nick, and Ryan, for being the amazing village to our family and providing us with endless and unconditional love and support, always.

To Mike, my life partner and best friend. There's never a doubt we were put on this earth to be together. Thank you for your unconditional love and support in me always. I'm so grateful to have my hubby also be my biggest cheerleader. I love you forever!

To Alyssa, Kate, and Scarlet, this book is for you three, and my hope is that no matter what life adversity you will face, you'll always know to come back to yourself and uncover your authentic power. I love you!

Dad, I focused on my mission and hope I made you proud.

RESOURCES

Anisha Abraham, M.D., M.P.H.
Author, *Raising Global Teens*
dranishaabraham.com

Suvrat Bhargave, M.D.
Author, *A Moment of Insight: Universal Lessons Learned from a Psychiatrist's Couch*
drbhargave.com

Amber Bodily
Master Herbalist, Medical Intuitive, and Footzoning Practitioner
amberbodilyhealth.com

Martha Calihan, M.D.
Author, *A Death Lived*
fivestoneswellness.com

Kushal Choski
The Art of Living / SKY Breathwork Facilitator
artofliving.org

Malena Crawford
Author, *A Fistful of Honey*
Founder, Black Divine Feminine Reawakened Movement
malenacrawford.com

Dan Deluca
Founder, Mindfulness in the Arts
mindfulnessinthearts.com

Dale DeNunzio, Ph.D., M.A., S.E.P.
Marriage and Family Therapy and Family Studies, and Somatic Experiencing (SE) Expert

Seku Gathers, M.D.
Host of the Truth Prescription podcast, Trauma Coach, and Former Emergency Room Physician
thetruthprescription.com

Jaime Hope, M.D.
Author, *Habit That!: How You Can Health Up in Just 5 Minutes a Day*
drhopehealth.com

Marci Moberg
Intuitive Coach and Healer
marcimoberg.com

Edy Nathan
Author, *It's Grief: The Dance
of Self-Discovery Through
Trauma and Loss*
edynathan.com

Claire Nicogossian, Psy.D.
Author, *Mama, You Are Enough*
drclairenicogossian.com
momswellbeing.com

Rajshree Patel
Author, *The Power of Vital Force*
rajshreepatel.com

Julie Reisler
Author, *Get a Ph.D. in You*
juliereisler.com

Annelies Richmond
Director of SKY Campus
Happiness Program and
Director of Teacher Training for
the Art of Living Foundation
www.skycampushappiness.org

Ocean Robbins
Author, *31-Day Food Revolution*
31dayfoodrevolution.com

Habib Sadeghi, D.O.
Author, *The Clarity Cleanse: 12
Steps to Finding Renewed Energy,
Spiritual Fulfillment, and
Emotional Healing*
behiveofhealing.com

LeeAnn Taylor
Author, *The Fragile Face of God*
leeanntaylor.com

**Dr. Marianne
Teitelbaum, D.C.**
Author, *Healing the Thyroid
with Ayurveda*
drmteitelbaum.com

**Chris Winfield &
Jen Gottlieb**
Founders, Super
Connector Media
superconnectormedia.com

Jamil Zaki, Ph.D.
Author, *The War for Kindness*
warforkindness.com